Glaen

A Novel Message on
Romance, Love, & Relating

Glaen

A Novel Message on
Romance, Love, & Relating

By

FRED R. LYBRAND

The Barnabas Agency

GLAEN
Published by The Barnabas Agency
a division of The B & B Media Group, Inc.
109 S. Main St., Corsicana, TX 75110 U.S.A.
www.barnabasagency.com

All scripture quotations, unless otherwise indicated, are taken from the New King James Version®. Copyright © 1982 by Thomas Nelson, Inc. Used by permission. All rights reserved.

LCCN: 2010920322
ISBN: 978-0-578-04652-5

Author is represented by the B & B Media Group, Inc.
109 S. Main St., Corsicana, TX 75110
1-800-927-0517
www.tbbmedia.com

Design: Lauri Worthington, Martino Creative

"Almost all of our sorrows spring out of
our relations with other people."

– Schopenhauer

Prologue

Here was our question, "How do you succeed in love and marriage?"

What you hold in your hands began several years ago as a couple of dad's debating our views on relationships and how to help our combined eleven children and all the unmarried people we know, both young and old. In time, we noticed that the principles we discovered helped our marriages, business relationships, and friendships too! No matter where we turned, relationships seemed to need help. Our deep conviction is that insight allows anyone to take new actions...and new actions often make the big difference.

It seemed a storyline would work best. I know these words, and this view, might raise more questions than answers; but when it comes to learning, questions are the ultimate tool.

I hope you find the love of your life, even if you need to do it all over again with the person you're already with. In any event, I don't offer myself as simply an expert, but more importantly I am a fellow sojourner in a life filled with relationships. I'm not only a husband and a father, but I'm also a veteran teen and a veteran single; once was unmarried and quite confused about the whole matter.

My suggestion is that you read this book through twice...once for the story, and again for the principles. Also, this may be just the thing for parents and kids to talk about together...buy your mom and dad their own copies! In fact, almost everyone will read this book if you hand it to them. And please, mark it up with under-lines, questions, and a few exclamation marks! We're learning here people.

Annie Hughes is a college student, who like many others, starts off behind the eight ball relationally. *Glaen* is unapologetically, but not uniquely, Christian in its slant. All human beings are relational creatures. Annie is sharing her take on the matters of romance, love, and relating. See if you can travel along with her to the answers you seek.

Mother called the week before I met Glaen Breuch.

"So, that's it?" I said with a tinge of anger.

"I'm afraid it is, dear," a soft and matter-of-fact voice responded.

"Mom, you just want a divorce? You don't want to work at it or get some counseling or something?" I pleaded.

"No Annie, it's over. I've tried and tried, but your father just isn't what I want for the rest of my life. Can't you just be happy for me?" Mother asked.

Suddenly Annie found herself floating, feather-like, away from the phone and experiencing what most people think a drowning person experiences; a life full of joy and promise, in the last moments of gasping for air, she sees a replay of that life. Annie saw the day her baby sister came home from the hospital. Mom and Dad were so happy, and Annie as a little girl couldn't find her sister's feet; she kept looking under the baby-carrier instead of under the blanket. They all laughed for days.

Next, Annie remembered her granddaddy's death and how her mother was so kind to her dad, and how her dad praised mother to everyone in the small town where he grew up. Other memories flooded her mind, moving from ancient black-and-white scenes to vivid full-color images. Most recently she had been in church, seated between her parents, and basking in the wonder of family; hoping for a marriage like theirs. But Annie snapped awake.

"Be happy for you?" I said with amazement. "How can I be happy for you? You are running away to ruin your relationship with Dad and mess up our family forever. You seem happy enough. I don't think you need my help."

"Annie, my relationship with your dad is already ruined. Honey, the one way I've failed you was to not really help you understand about love. You were always your Daddy's girl anyway, so I never could really tell you how I felt. I don't think I understand relationships, but I'm going to learn about them. Honey, I know you don't understand relationships; just look at what's happened with your boyfriends."

"Boyfriends?" Annie thought to herself. There were just two; one in high school and one in college. Both of the boys were nice guys who doted, and spent, on Annie. She just wanted to have fun, and she did, for a while. In the same six month period with each guy, Rodney and Pierre, they both turned to the same serious conversation with her about "dating just each other." Annie could still feel the panic as her stomach tightened and her lungs closed off from the air in the room. She had mysteriously decided she didn't like either of them; and in time she believed it deeply. The only hint she had that perhaps a mistake lived on, was that she saved the letter from Pierre in her dresser drawer back home. Both guys were married now, at least she had heard about their engagements. But now the thought of her past brought Annie back to the room, and to the moment.

"Mother, what about your relationship with God? What about your marriage vow before Him?" I asked as a sincere question.

"God wants us happy, dear. I've been miserable for years. I love you children, and now that you're grown, I can follow my dreams. I felt dead, but now I feel alive. Annie, I know it is hard to understand, but I just know God is in this because I'm so wonderfully happy now."

"Mom...I love you, but what you're doing can't be right. I'm not going to do this to my family," I said.

"Well, good luck, Honey. I'm going out to dinner and I haven't finished dressing," she said in a mother-knows-best way.

"Could I give you one piece of advice that would have changed all of this for me?"

"Sure Mom," I said.

"Annie dear, be sure you marry the right person; don't stand in your wedding dress with doubts in your bouquet."

We hung up, and I cried for a long time before I could pray. "God, my mother says she doesn't understand relationships, and she's my mom! Then she says I don't understand them either. Please help me to understand."

Back then I had no idea that prayer was the sort of thing God took seriously.

Glaen Breuch was unusual, even for a college professor.

It was only two weeks before that I had signed up for his Masters class called, "Original Non-Fiction." Jennah and I had been sitting at Polmier's Coffee Shoppe, a little place with hardwood floors full of serious students and a few silly girls. "What are you going to take for your last class?" Jennah asked. I was irritated. "Gee, Jennah, I just decided now to take classes at all." She knew how upset I was about Mom and Dad's sudden divorce announcement, so she ignored it and asked again.

"I've prayed all week about it. I wish I could take a class on how relationships really work, but nothing in school is ever practical." I still remember saying those words when Glaen walked in the Shoppe. He had striking white hair that made a great wave until it crashed above his right eye. Wire-rimmed glasses, herringbone jacket, too many books; all these made Glaen look like the ideal professor. He insisted on being called Glaen rather than "professor" or "mister," but I didn't know why until months later.

Exactly fifteen years ago I saw Glaen in the Shoppe. Now I am about to see him again. I bet he hasn't changed a bit, but of course how could he?

That day in Polmier's, Glaen walked up to us as an answer to prayer. "Hi ladies," he said. "I couldn't help overhearing your conversation about classes. I'm a new instructor here at St. Michael's, but I'm a bit late in arriving." Suddenly his awkward grasp gave way and all of his books and papers clamored to the wood floor. Only one pink sheet remained in his hand. "Oh, here it is," ignoring the pile at his feet. "I'm teaching this class over the next two semesters. If you're interested, just show up as it says here." With that Glaen gathered his books and left the Shoppe, cluttered but unembarrassed. From that moment on, all I could think about was how curious both the class and the professor seemed. I was in!

"Welcome class. My name is Glaen, pronounced with a long 'a' as in 'gain.'" He started the Original Non-Fiction class, ONF-101 as the flier labeled it, right on time. Without skipping a beat he handed out the syllabus and asked with eyes that swept the room, "Are there any questions before we begin?"

I looked around totally bewildered as I raised my hand. "Yes, and your name is Anne?" he asked. "Well, they call me Annie, but I do have a question," I said.

"OK Annie, what's your question?" I was still in a self-absorbed mood, so I put a little "dumb blonde" in my voice. "Like...ah...I'm the only student in the room...and, ah...is the class going to make or something?" I wanted to ask why in heaven's name he was acting like the room was full, but it seemed like a dumb move on the first day.

"Well Annie, since it's a new class the powers-that-be have given me permission to teach it even if you're the only one. Ready to start?" he asked, taking my silence for a "yes."

Glaen wrote the following on the board and asked, "What do you think?"

"JUST DEFINITIONS EITHER PREVENT OR PUT AN END TO DISPUTES"

– Emmons

"Who's Emmons?" I said.

"Does it matter? What if I said it was written by Poe, or Shelley, or Whitman? Would it make a difference? Is it what is said or who said it?" suddenly Glaen had me thinking.

"I guess it doesn't matter," I said.

"Then what do you think?" he returned.

"I think it sounds reasonable," I admitted.

"Great!" Glaen took off with a quick lecture on the importance of words and their meanings. He finally got to the point.

"Annie, I've watched conflict for a long time. Seldom is there a conflict that can withstand agreed-to definitions. The reason is pretty simple: Truth still wins out. It's bad enough when two people disagree about what is expected in a relationship. It's even worse when they aren't using the same language. A dictionary or the question, 'What do you mean?' can do more to end conflict than almost anything else on the planet. One of my favorite authors once wrote, '**Truth is the lifeblood of real relationships.**'"

"Why?" I asked.

"Well, let me ask you a question. If you change your behavior from how you really are to what they want; is it you relating, or is it the character you're playing?"

With that Glaen started to put his books in a much-needed satchel.

"Is that it?" I asked.

"There's nothing else to know for today," he said.

"Nothing else to know! What about non-fiction? What about writing? What's the assignment?" I said with a little contempt.

"Oh, that," he said flatly.

"Well, you need to write an original work of non-fiction, offering original insights on a useful topic. It doesn't matter what the topic is, but I would suggest you write about something you care about, something you'd like to understand. I'll be in this room every week at this same moment. I'm available to help you when you want it."

Glaen looked at me for a long time, staring right through me with his steady blue eyes, framed by his white hair and white button-down shirt.

"Annie," he added. "Decide on your topic by next week and I'll show you the secret of good non-fiction. There's a book in your future, and I want to show it to you." Glaen turned and moved out of the room with the grace of a ballet dancer. I just sat there for a long time before I left. The Coffee Shoppe was finally calling.

SUMMARY

Truth is the lifeblood of real relationships.

"Theory 1 and Theory 2?" Jennah asked.

"Yes!" I said. "He told me I could write about anything. I think Theory 1 and Theory 2 need to be put to the test."

"What are you talking about?" she said as she reminded me I was a little ahead in my thinking.

"Oh yeah, sorry," I said as I hurried to explain myself. "I'm talking about dating and marriage and lasting relationships."

"Two chocolate mocha mint coffees, frothed, and extra whipped cream," Jake said as he placed our orders on the table.

"Keep your day job, Jake. Comedy's not your thing," Jennah said with a smile. Jake knew we had sworn off whipped cream for the summer sun-worshipping our waists required.

"Just sharing the truth I see," Jake mused as he walked back to the coffee bar.

Jennah and I both sat frozen before bursting into laughter. Jake was right, but we played with him because he's one of the good guys. We first met Jake at H.O.W., which means Heart of Worship; a campus club that sponsors a weekly Bible Study and worship concert. Jake spoke one evening about temptation. He said from working at Polmier's, he had observed a difference between guys and girls. "Guys," he said, "lust for women…but women lust for chocolate!" Of course we all roared because it's truer than we'd like to admit. "Just sharing the truth I see" was the last line of his talk before quoting 1 Corinthians 10:13,

> No temptation has overtaken you except such as
> is common to man, but God is faithful, who will
> not allow you to be tempted beyond what you are able,
> but with the temptation will also make the way of
> escape, that you may be able to bear it.

Jake told us that the Greek word for "temptation" is often translated as "trial" in the Bible. I know I sat there and thought about my current trial; my parents' divorce. "God will show me the way out of the trial, the temptation?" My only temptation was to have nothing to do with guys–to avoid marriage at all costs.

"Annie? Annie?" Jennah was tapping me on the arm.

"Theory 1 and Theory 2?" she asked.

"Oh, sorry," I said.

"Jennah, my temptation is to bail out on relationships, especially the guy/girl kind."

"But Annie," she interrupted.

"I know," I continued. "I'm not saying I'm going to–I just WANT to! Remember how Jake told us that God will provide the way out? I think He has." I suddenly was whispering, not because it was a secret, but because God's work in our lives seems kinda sacred.

"I think God wants me to write a book about relationships between Christian women and men. I especially want to discover how to see relationships grow and last a lifetime. Mom and Dad's divorce is only a part of my interest. I love them, but they weren't exactly church-goers when they met." Mom and Dad were a little different than the normal fairy tale. They were introduced on a blind date. Dad is really brilliant, but not the most dashing attorney in town. Mom is attractive, but given to a lot of spontaneous decision-making. On the second date they got "plastered," as they tell it, and wound up in bed together. They figured since they had had sex, they must be in love…and…

"Annie, focus here. Theory 1 and Theory 2?" poor Jennah persisted.

"Thanks friend," I told her. "I see two ways to 'date' as a Christian couple. One I call Theory 1, and the other, Theory 2. Like a scientific experiment, I want to see which one makes for the best relationship."

"So what's Theory 1?" Jennah asked.

"Theory 1 is what you and Trevor are doing," I said.

"You mean having a good time getting to know each other by dating?" she added.

"Yes, but it's more than that. Are you guys dating anyone else?" I asked.

"No."

"Would it be OK with you if Trevor went out with someone else?"

"No!" Jennah said emphatically.

"Do you expect him to put you first in his life?"

"Of course."

"And if he decides to spend Saturday night with his friends instead of being with you?"

"That would be so inconsiderate!'"

"Inconsiderate of whom? Never mind. Would you marry him if he asked you?" I probed a little more.

"I don't know, I guess maybe I would."

"Jennah, it sounds like you already think you are married!" I said.

Jennah just smiled and finished her coffee. "We're not through with school yet; it isn't time to talk about marriage," she protested.

"Whatever. Here's another question: How many guys have you seriously dated in your life?" I asked.

After a long pause Jennah said, "Six."

"Six," I nodded. "Don't you wonder if the guy before last was the right one?"

"No way! He was bitter and hurtful when I broke it off. Hey, I don't like this conversation. I'm just trying to fall in love, get married, and have a life," Jennah said sharply.

"I know, Jennah. I'm just saying that as Christians we are trying to follow God's design of one man, for one woman, for life. Can it make sense that date-break-up, date-break-up, date-break-up will actually teach us about commitment?"

"It sounds like you already have your mind made up, Annie. Are you really going to give dating a chance? I mean, no offense, but you don't seem to be on a path toward marriage at all and…what would you want me to do?"

"My mom said about the same thing," I replied, feeling more and more inadequate by the moment. "If Theory 1 holds up, then

that's great, and I will give it a chance, because I really don't
know what else to do. But I might think about trying Theory 2."

"What's Theory 2?" Jennah mumbled.

"I'll tell you later, I'm late for my Renaissance Seminar. Hello
to Trevor!" I shouted as I left the Shoppe. I couldn't help thinking
how touchy she was about the whole thing. "Maybe this project
wasn't going to be received as warmly as I hoped," I thought on
the way. Little did I know how hot the topic was, or would be.

Relationship Field Book Journal
Dating:
" having a good time getting to know
each other"
(referring to guy & girl)
—Jennah

So began my notes on relationships. Jennah had supplied my
first practical definition.

"There," I thought. Glaen said to start keeping notes on
what I was learning. This had to be a good start.

Theory 1: Traditional Dating

A process by which a girl and guy get to know each other through a period of time spent in different settings to see if they fall in love and want to get married. Marriage may be in view, it is for Jennah, but the path there seems a bit obscure. It seems that these relationships often take on aspects of marriage such as exclusiveness and intimate physical affection, but in practice most often end in a painful rejection by one of the participants toward the other. And then, the cycle repeats...in hope that a relationship finally makes it into marriage.

I reflected that Jennah seems to view her current relationship like the hoped for "happily ever after" tale, but actually she has endured a misery cycle. But that was exactly how Jennah represented Theory 1; so there it is, and there would be much time to pursue the possibilities. So I decided to analyze it later, and next I wrote:

Theory 2: Courting

...An old-fashioned prelude to marriage being re-popularized by some Christians. Courting is defined by Webster's as, "to engage in social activities leading to engagement and marriage."

Since I don't really know about it, I wonder who I can talk to?

"Hi, I'm Annie," I said to the couple standing next to Jake. Jake made the introductions and we sat down after he took our orders. "So, how did you two meet?" I asked.

"We met at SummitView, which is a pre-college training our denomination puts on to prepare kids for the challenges to their faith they'll face in school," Ken, the six-foot sandy-blonde with dark-rimmed glasses said.

"It turned out we bumped into each other again at our first H.O.W. meeting, but it was two years before we started courting," Bette, the brunette with a huge smile, added as she looked at Ken.

"Well," I said. "As Jake told you, I'm starting to work on a class project about dating and marriage. I've heard about courting, but I wanted someone who really understands it to explain it to me. Can you help?"

Ken and Bette smiled as they nodded. "Sure," Ken said. "Bette introduced me to the idea of courting when she told me about a conference she had attended. Basically, it begins with a rejection of 'dating' as a concept. Dating must be rejected because it tends to be a 'serial' event, like a serial killer. You go from one relationship to another leaving a trail of hurt, or carrying a lot of scars yourself. Also, since marriage is not necessarily a part of the dating mindset, it invites sexual involvement, something we want to save for marriage," Ken finished as Jake showed up with our coffee.

"Wait a minute," I interrupted. "You mean if you date you'll have sex? That seems to be a bit of a leap, doesn't it?"

"We're not saying that you'll have sex if you date," Bette said. "We're saying that since marriage is not in view, waiting will not make sense over time. For Christians who choose to delay sex until marriage there isn't a purpose or deadline in view, so where does a relationship centered on romance have to go? Really, there isn't a way to think about it. If you're just dating and pursuing romance to have fun, fun will likely include sex, since sex is progressive in nature. If sex has a purpose in the long-term relationship, then waiting can work. If sex is just for fun, the relationship will hardly matter."

"So, if you're dating rather than courting, sex will be a big temptation," I summarized.

"Well put," Ken smiled.

"What else does courting involve?" I asked.

"Since courting is a strategy for marriage, it has three basic requirements that should be met; financial, emotional, and spiritual."

"Wow," I said a little tongue-in-cheek. "Are you saying that you should be grown up to get married?"

Bette laughed, "Wouldn't it have been great if our parents were grown up when they raised us?"

I got a little quiet before Ken added a word.

"Stability," Ken said. "Stability financially. Stability emotionally. And, stability spiritually. Those are the prerequisites, along with the support of your parents and church leaders."

Journal Entry

We finished talking in about an hour and I had to confess, what they shared sounded pretty cool. Ken had met with Bette's dad at her request. Ken explained that he wanted to court Bette, but only with her folks' agreement. He also made it clear that the long-term goal was marriage; and that courting would be a way for God to confirm His will to everyone involved. Bette said her dad got to share his expectations with Ken regarding the relationship as well.

They're making wedding plans and career plans. They both want to pursue full-time ministry and plan to attend their denomination's seminary. I can't help but think how great it would be to enter into a life-long relationship that well prepared. It is amazing to me that they got this far without seeming to have first gotten to know one another very well. Anyway, it looks like they've got it together; financially stable, emotionally stable, and spiritually stable. It sounds like a winning strategy! I wonder what Glaen will think of what I've got so far?

Glaen was right on time.

"So, have you decided?" he asked.

"Yes!" I replied, "I want to write my book about relationships, dating, and marriage."

"Sounds great," he said as he walked to the board and wrote the word "Tension."

"What are you going to give your reader?" he asked.

After I explained Theory 1 and Theory 2, Glaen looked at me with a funny half-smile and said, "What if neither Theory works?"

I remember thinking, "Well, what other options are there except rolling dice? And besides, you haven't even met Ken and Bette." Instead I said, "What's tension?"

"Ah," Glaen said. "Tension is your friend." He stared for a long time past me, out the window, toward the sky.

Finally I asked, "Why? Or…How?"

"Hmm," Glaen began. "Have you ever watched a movie or read a novel such that you've come to a place you can't stop, and you won't let anyone or anything keep you from finishing?"

"Sure," I said.

"Why?" Glaen asked.

"I wanted to finish it." I said emphatically.

"Why?" he smiled.

"I don't know. I just wanted to," I said.

"Exactly!" He shouted loud enough for the whole world to hear. "You have been designed for tension. Every sporting event succeeds or fails because of tension. Ratings drop when a golfer or tennis star is too dominant or too far in the lead. Movies fail when they are too easy to figure out. People don't even vote when their candidate is going to easily win…or lose. Human beings love tension, even though they claim to hate it. Also Annie, it's not really the tension they love, it's the feeling resolution brings that's so incredible. What happened to you when I wrote 'tension' on the board?"

"I started wondering why it was on the board," I said.

"And what did you do?" Glaen asked.

"I asked about it?" I offered.

"Exactly!" he said. "Which is really interesting because you avoided the tension I created by asking you about the possibility of Theory 1 and Theory 2 both being wrong."

"I didn't have an answer, so I...."

"You eased the tension by moving to a different topic," Glaen interrupted.

"So I was trying to resolve the two tensions that were right in front of me?" I asked.

"Exactly," Glaen beamed.

"Annie, most humans miss out on learning and growing because they don't hold on to the tension long enough. They resolve it by quitting, or guessing, or changing tensions. Tension is WHY people keep reading books, both fiction and non-fiction. When you understand this fact, you'll know the secret to writing good non-fiction. Here's your assignment: Come back next class and explain the difference between fiction and non-fiction, and how tension works in each."

With that Glaen said his goodbye and passed through the door.

"How is this going to help me understand dating and relationships?" I yelled down the hall to Glaen.

"You don't think relationships are about tension and resolution?" he echoed back to me.

I felt like a selfish pig. I had spent so much time wallowing in my own despair about my parents' divorce that I hadn't even thought about Krista. I phoned her as soon as I could stop the merry-go-round of my schedule. Krista, my baby sister, was as hurt as I was, and we shared tears for a while. I made a mental promise to start phoning her weekly. I decided to focus on her everyday life, like I had when I lived at home. Of course, given her age, the conversation always turned to boys. But now I had a new interest in the subject.

"Don't you want to know who I like?" asked Krista. I knew this wasn't a real question.

"Who is it?" I asked, instinctively glancing at my watch to see how long I had before I needed to leave for H.O.W.

"Well, Marsha Steeples—do you remember Marsha? Well, Marsha came and told me that Mike Blakely liked me! Can you believe it? Mike Blakely!" she beamed with her voice.

"I don't remember Mike Blakely," I replied. The minutes ticked away as I heard about the wonders of Mike Blakely. Something kept haunting me in the back of my mind as she sang her praise-to-Mike song. As she continued, Glaen came to mind. Definitions! Just definitions prevent or end disputes!

"Krista," I said, when I got a chance to stop her. "What did Marsha mean when she said that Mike 'liked' you?"

I could almost see her eyes roll as she sighed. "I guess Mom is right, you don't know anything about relationships," she said rather clipped. "Ouch, that hurt," I thought to myself.

"Really, Krista, I'm doing a project in school about dating and marriage and romance. I'm really interested. What did you think when you heard that Mike 'liked' you?"

"It was exciting, Annie. Mike is really popular, and just think, he likes me!" she said.

"So I guess you didn't already like him? Why is it different now that you know he likes you?"

"Why's it different? Annie, don't you know anything? Everything's different."

I thought about Glaen's lesson on "tension" and wondered if he was thinking about talking to a fifteen-year-old. I laughed at the thought, but stopped as I realized I was just trying to seek "resolution" with Krista. So, I tried to change my approach, but nothing worked. Krista just insisted that everyone gets it.

"Annie, it's not hard to understand. He just likes me, and now I like him. Everybody knows how it works. You would do a lot better if you didn't try to analyze everything to death," she said. Just like Mom.

After we hung up I realized there is more to relating than I first guessed; and that getting clear definitions is harder than you think.

You can tell when someone's been crying. Jennah sat with her back to the door at Polmier's. No book was open, no coffee ordered. She just sat there with a wad of tissue in her left hand.

"What's wrong?" I said as I quietly sat across from her.

"It's seven, now," she said.

"Seven what?" I replied.

"You asked me how many guys had I seriously dated, and I said, 'Six.'"

"So you and Trevor broke up?" I asked as Jennah nodded and started crying all over again. "What happened?"

"He came over for dinner," she began. "We were just talking and I brought up the project you're working on; you know, Theory 1 and Theory 2. Well, it got us talking about commitment and marriage, then suddenly Trevor blew up about how I'm pressuring him and expect him to be with me every minute of the day. Annie, I've never tried to pressure Trevor...I've tried to be understanding when he'd go out with his friends and leave me stuck at my apartment alone." Jennah paused to cry, and breathe.

"I know, sweetie," I tried to comfort her. "But that doesn't sound like the end of the relationship."

"Trevor told me he's been seeing somebody else. When I asked him, 'Who?' he said it didn't matter and that we should date other people to make sure we're right for each other."

After a while I left Jennah for class, and even though I felt terrible for her, all I could think about was the number of times we had talked about how mad she was at Trevor for not spending more time with her. "If tension seeks resolution, then I guess Trevor found relief in getting away from Jennah," I thought to myself.

Journal Entry

As I work on the class project about relationships, I get the feeling that there's something obvious I keep missing. Jennah was so caught up in trying to get Trevor to do what she wanted, she couldn't (or didn't) see what was going on. It's just like Mom and Dad. If Mom had hushed her constant complaining, Dad might have listened. Of course, if he had spent any time telling Mom what he actually thought instead of being so "nice," they might have been able to really discuss things. It's like neither one would behave quite right for the other one ...

Tension Seeks Resolution
Assignment: Figure out the difference between fiction and non-fiction concerning *Tension Seeks Resolution*

At Glaen's suggestion, I've studied some of the works of Robert Fritz and am getting the idea that this is a basic principle of God's universe. Simply, it looks like I read a work of fiction and keep wondering, "What's next... and...then what?" With non-fiction (they are "How To" or "What to know" books) it's different. With non-fiction I often don't finish the book after I've read a lot of it...I don't need to, because ...

<u>Of Course!</u>

At that moment the phone rang with a weeping Jennah on the other end. It wouldn't matter though, I just figured out the secret of writing non-fiction. I couldn't wait to see Glaen.

[1] Robert Fritz, the originator of structural dynamics, has authored several best-selling books, including *The Path of Least Resistance, Creating,* and *Your Life as Art*.

"Been playing all night?" Glaen said without looking up.

"Playing…praying, whatever," I told him. "My friend Jennah, who you saw at the Coffee Shoppe, just broke up with the guy she'd hoped to marry."

"Humans take that stuff pretty hard, don't they?" Glaen mused.

"We do," I said. "It's why I want to figure out the secret to good relationships."

"First things first, Annie," he said. "What about non-fiction and tension? After all, what good is finding the secret if no one reads the book?"

"I know how it works," I stated outright.

"Go on," Glaen said, believing me. Glaen always seemed to have faith in me, which felt wrong for a while; especially when he showed me a copy of The Book.

"Well, it seems simple now. Movies and fictional stories have some character you start cheering for, but who runs into conflicts which keep him from getting what he wants. For example, in the old movie It's a Wonderful Life, Jimmy Stewart's character wants to leave his crummy little town and explore the world. Instead, every time he tries to leave something happens like the Great Depression.

His own good nature stops him each time. He can't even leave town by committing suicide. God sends an angel to stop him and help him see how important his life has been to so many.

"Anyway, throughout the movie, you keep watching and wondering, 'What's next?' That's the tension. You keep watching or reading to find out what happens." I finished and caught my breath.

"Nice." Glaen said. "And what about non-fiction?"

"That's trickier," I said, not knowing if trickier was even a word. "I thought about books and magazines which explain how to do something, and why I read them. The funny thing is that I usually don't finish them. Until meeting you I thought I was lazy or undisciplined. Now I know its just tension-seeks-resolution. *I'm finished with fiction when I know what happened. I'm finished with non-fiction when I learn what I want to learn.* A few weeks ago I was so mad because I bought a magazine that I didn't finish. It had an article about different types of braids. When I opened it at my apartment, the centerfold had diagrams which explained how to braid my hair. That was all I needed, but I spent a week trying to make myself read articles about which vegetables cause the greatest release of pheromones to attract my perfect mate. All I need in my life is to attract 'carrot man.'"

Even Glaen laughed at that. "I got all I wanted. My tension was 'how to braid,' and the resolution was the diagram. I had no desire to read after that." I tried to add a few more thoughts, but Glaen abruptly shut me off.

"Annie, what's the tension you want to resolve for your readers?"

"Glaen," I said, "I want my readers to know how relationships really work; what makes them flounder, what makes them thrive, and how to find the right mate, et cetera."

While I was answering the question Glaen had packed up, and silently as if floating, moved out into the hall where I heard his voice call back to me, "Do you know what you want your readers to know?"

I think I sat there for thirty minutes looking at my yellow pad before I answered him. "Not yet Glaen," I mumbled. "Not just yet."

"Hi, Bette, this is Annie, Annie Hughes. I met you and your fiancé at Polmier's one day to talk about courting. Do you remember me?" I shifted my phone to my left ear so I could write.

"Well, I was wondering how things are going?" I said.

Bette spoke and I fell into my television chair.

"You're kidding!" I said with astonishment. "I'm so sorry," and just like that, the call ended.

Basically my "courting" couple was finished. I checked around through a few friends and found out that she had called it off. Apparently, as they moved closer to the wedding, after a shower, and presents, and invitations, etc., Bette started to find out Ken had a secret life involving some emotional challenges, prescription drugs, and another "girlfriend" at Briercrest Junior College about twenty miles away. He was very broken, and very committed, to doing whatever it would take to keep on track toward marriage. Bette, however, took her dad's advice. As hard as it was, her dad recommended postponing the wedding until she was sure about her relationship with Ken. Apparently Ken blew up and the relationship ended for good.

"Now what do I do?" I thought aloud. "I was skeptical that Theory 1 would offer a concrete solution to effective relationships, and it didn't. It seems that Theory 2 makes a lot of sense as a path toward marriage. But neither seems to give an answer to how to make relationships really work. Maybe relationships just operate randomly. Maybe they should add commitment to their courting list. Maybe relationships can't be guaranteed, or just don't work at all!"

I sat there with one-half of the year gone and nothing to write about. I remember thinking how useless an original non-fiction book entitled, *A Great Relationship: The Impossible Dream* would be to Christians, or to anybody else for that matter.

"Maybe I should just quit. I still got an A for the first semester," I thought. I was stuck, and knew if God wanted me to write something useful He'd better send my guardian angel with a few answers.

Glaen was a little more relaxed than normal. His feet were propped up, his chair tilted back, and he was engrossed in a book. He just rocked back-and-forth occasionally saying, "Hmm...hmm...yes!"

"Uh, Glaen?" I asked along with clearing my throat.
"I'm here."

"You ever heard of my friend, Isaac Newton?" Glaen blurted out.

"You mean the guy with the apple hitting his head and discovering the Laws of Motion?" I said.

"The same," Glaen returned.

"Yes, why?" I said.

"Most people don't understand what he really did, Annie."

"What's that?" I asked, mildly interested.

"Well, Newton was able to see with such clarity, that he put together his insights with extreme accuracy. NASA uses some of his math even now, three hundred years later, to put space shuttles in orbit. Annie, do you know how he did it?"

"Not really," I said, suddenly seeing a geeky-side of Glaen I didn't want to know about.

"Listen to what Charles Van Doren says in his book,
A History of Knowledge:

> Newton loathed hypotheses. He saw in them all the
> egregious and harmful errors of the past.
> . . . The most important thing he did not know was
> the cause or causes of gravitation. That the earth and
> the other planets were held in their courses by the sun's
> gravity he had no doubt, but he did not know why. But
> "I frame no hypotheses," he declared; "for whatever is
> not deduced from the phenomena is to be called a
> hypothesis, and hypotheses 'have no place' in science."

"Annie, what he did was to refuse to guess. He only wanted
to observe, to discover, rather than to invent theories about how
things should work."

"Glaen, that's my problem," I interrupted.

"What's that?" Glaen asked as he put the book down and
leaned forward.

"Do you remember Theory 1 and Theory 2?" I didn't wait for
his response. "Neither has given me any real answers about how
relationships work. I thought if I found the right process I would
discover how they work. Now I don't know what to do. I don't
have any idea what to say about relationships. I don't even know
if they really can work."

"That's wonderful," Glaen beamed in a way I knew he
was serious.

"Annie, you are at a really cool and really delicate place. You're teachable."

"Teachable?" I thought. "Doesn't he mean ignorant or stupid?"

Glaen went on, "Annie, teachable is when you're willing to unlearn so you can really learn. Most people are trying to prove their theories about how the world should work. You have an opportunity to be the Isaac Newton of relationships."

I suddenly felt like I was starting to catch a cold of Glaen's geekiness.

"What do you mean?" I asked.

"Miss Hughes, Isaac Newton had two things working for him. First, as best he could, he refused theories; he focused on making honest observations. When the apple hit him, he noticed it fell. He observed that some force drew it to the ground. If it were today, most people would think the apple tree had it in for them."

"What's the second thing?" I asked.

"The second thing was Newton's faith."

"His faith?" I asked a little irritated. "Isn't faith just another word for theory?"

"No, Annie. Faith has a basis, while theories search for a basis. It's the difference between trusting and guessing."

Glaen looked off for a long minute before he continued. "Hebrews 11:1 in your Bible says,

Now faith is the substance of things hoped for, the evidence of things not seen.

Annie, Isaac Newton was a man of observation, or science. However, he was also a man of faith, faith in God. He believed God was the great designer or architect of the Universe; so if he could see, really see, with his observations how God designed things to be, then he could understand how God made things to work. It was because he believed in God that he simply took an honest look at the way things truly worked."

"So you're saying…" I interrupted. "If I can honestly observe relationships, and have faith that God designed a way they truly work, I'll discover what I'm looking for?"

"Exactly!"

"Do I have to believe in God to discover it?" I asked.

"No," Glaen smiled, "Just a designer."

"OK. I really, really want to know how God designed relationships to work, so where do I start?"

Glaen smiled and said, "Annie, I think you should start with faith, like Newton did. I'm not allowed to help you, but I can give you a place to start."

With that Glaen wrote on a piece of paper, folded it, and dropped it in my purse.

"After you get your faith in place we'll learn how to observe," Glaen said as he floated down the hall.

"OK," I said. "Faith first."

"There you go; one un-decaffeinated coffee," Jake said as he placed the Polmier's cup in front of the folded paper.

"What are you doing, Annie? I mean; black coffee, no company, and you're staring at a note?" Jake asked.

"I'm doing homework," I muttered.

"Nice," he said. "Is it a Zen thing where you think you are the note?"

I smiled because Jake always seemed to know how to make the ridiculous seem absurd.

"I'm trying to understand faith," I said.

"Is that like trying to see the sound of silence?" he offered.

Suddenly I got it. "Wow, Jake, I think you just helped me get an 'A' on this assignment!"

"Glad I could help. Could you clue me in? I'd like to know what I did," he said.

"Well when you just said, 'see the sound of silence,' I realized that what I'm trying to do is impossible. I can't really see sound or hear silence. And I don't think it's possible to completely understand faith by means of reason."

"Sounds reasonable," Jake piped in. "What about faith?"

"Well," I said. "It looks like faith operates more from the heart than the head. Faith is often reasonable, but it can also not make sense, at least not in the way that we can know first hand. Faith in God is a good example. Someone can logically conclude that the existence of the universe insists on a brilliant Creator. However, a rational admission isn't really faith. When someone believes in God they kind of 'know' He's there tending to the universe, and listening to their individual prayers. You sort of believe what you believe, which isn't unreasonable, but it can't really submit to the rules of reason or science either." I finished and looked at Jake for a moment. "Wow!" I said. "The caffeine seems to be taking over."

"No, that's good," Jake said. "I've noticed that we Christians hold a lot of faith in the future promises of the Bible. We can't really prove that faith in Jesus Christ gives us heaven, because we can't check it out until we die. If we could, then it wouldn't be faith anymore."

"Great point, Jake!" I said. "When we're there and see heaven, we can't believe any more, because then we'll know by experience."

"Nice. So what's the paper?" Jake pointed to Glaen's note, which I still hadn't opened.

"That's from my professor. I'm sure it has something to do with faith and the project I'm working on. I wanted to understand a little better what believing was all about before I opened it."

"So that explains the Zen moment with the coffee and the gaze at the note," Jake observed.

"Yep. You wanna open it?" I said.

"Annie, I'm about to get fired. Just tell me when you finish. I'll be around."

With that Jake went back to work and I just stared at the note. "OK, Glaen. What do I need to know about faith so I can discover about relationships what Isaac Newton discovered about gravity," I said quietly, reaching for the paper. I slowly unfolded the note to see in Glaen's beautiful script, the following:

> But without faith it is impossible to please Him, for he who comes to God must believe that He is, and that He is a rewarder of those who diligently seek Him.
> Hebrews 11:6

Two days after reading Glaen's note I met with Jennah for our weekly discipleship time.

"Hi, Jennah! How's it going since the breakup?" I asked.

"Well, I haven't seen my Ex at all. I hear he's being a player these days, but I don't really care…."

"You don't care?" I said. "We stayed up for hours that first night trying to keep you from giving up on ever having a good life! You said, 'That's it…there's no hope…I hate guys!' Jenn, what happened? Did you decide to become a nun?"

"Better than that, Annie!" Jennah said. "God brought me the neatest guy! You know I'm finally taking my language require-ment...well, in Spanish I met Jeremy. He's from Maine and has traveled throughout Europe. We've sat by each other in class all semester, but suddenly I noticed him; and, well, I really did want a little help with class... Anyway, we went for coffee after class and he was so nice! He talked, really talked, and listened to me! I've forgotten what it's like to have a guy really listen to me–I just think he may be the one!"

I'm sure if Jennah could have seen what I was thinking behind my eyes, she would have run away. Here was my dear friend going from her supposed life partner, to a break up and despair, to love again in a matter of weeks! I've heard it said that insanity is doing the same thing over and over again, but expecting different results. Well, there she was again!

I listened to her talk for a while and sat there debating whether or not I should say anything. I thought, "She'd just get upset, and finally, she's happy." As I sat there, half involved in the lesson, and half involved in worrying about Jennah; I felt these words in my heart, "...speaking the truth in love...speak truth one to another." It began to overwhelm me and I argued with it. They were Bible verses I had studied. They were from Ephesians. They were talking about sound teaching. They were not about shooting straight with Jennah.

Soon I couldn't help it. "Jenn," I said. "Could I ask you a question?"

"Sure," she said.

"Jennah, why is this time different?"

"What do you mean?" she asked.

"Jenn," I said. "How many times have you quickly fallen for a guy, become convinced he's the one, and started getting mad when you don't get enough attention, to finally see it end?"

Jennah got really quiet and then whispered, "It's never worked."

"So why do you keep trying when it never works for you?"

"I don't know another way, and I really want to get married and have a family," she said.

"But don't you want to marry somebody who's right for you?" I asked.

"Sure, but how can I find him if I don't keep trying?"

"Jenn, I don't know; but by God's mercy, Glaen, and Isaac Newton, I plan to find out! Want to help me?"

"Sure. I'm tired of failing. It makes me feel crazy."

I couldn't help but think that hope began to spring fresh that night.

"I'm sorry, run that past me again," I said to the ever-cryptic Glaen.

"Well, let me see if I can say it another way," he offered.

"Everything's hard before it's easy...."

"And everything's easy once you know how," I chimed in, nodding my head up and down.

"So," Glaen said. "You should get it! Annie, you don't know how to see what you're looking at; it's a skill you haven't developed yet. You don't have to get to Newton's level because the Lord made relationships more obvious than the physics behind the creation. All you need to do is get to a place where you can see the obvious."

"So, how do I do that?" I asked.

"Practice, practice, practice," Glaen said.

"I know, I know," I added. "Practice makes perfect."

"Not always," Glaen said. "Practice makes permanent. If you practice in the wrong way it just creates a really bad habit. But, if you improve as you practice, it makes for the skill you can use in an instant. Annie, if you want to see what's really happening in relationships, you've got to see them in an instant! Get it?" Glaen asked.

"I get it," I said a little subdued. "But, what do I practice?"

"I've written it down on this note," Glaen said as he handed it to me. "But this time, don't stare at it, practice it."

"OK, Glaen. I'm off to practice," I said as I finally left the room one time before Glaen.

"Annie," Glaen said as I got to the classroom door. "You need a subject matter for the note." After a long pause he said, "I suggest you observe what it is that makes certain girls attractive to certain guys…Oh, and write down what you notice."

I was outside with the bright sun bearing down on Glaen's note when I opened it and read it. Beautiful handwriting offered these words:

The more you look
the more you see

She walked into Polmier's with a tight white sweater, apple-red lips, and earrings that dangled and glittered noisily around the Shoppe. She also was as blonde as they come. So far, observing wasn't that tough. Two guys at the back table glanced at her, poked each other, and seemed to snicker as they looked down at their books. They were probably in engineering or computers; they had loose clothes, sandals, and stringy hair.

Next, a couple of guys walked in who were not in school; except maybe in the school of rough-riding. One had a tattoo of a star or a fish which ran up under his T-shirt. The other looked about the same. I'm pretty sure they used the word "Harley" every day. They walked past her, right past her, and didn't even notice she was there. They just kept hitting each other and laughed while they ordered. The good news was that she didn't notice them either.

After a few notes to myself about how boring observing seems, in walked an Australian tennis player. Well, maybe he wasn't either one, but he looked the part. He had sandy hair and a perfect complexion…and smile. They apparently were a couple. He leaned into her and whispered. She leaned into him and laughed. I also noticed how she would roll her eyes upward, bat her lashes, and smile–all in a movement away from the Aussie, which called him to follow…and he leaned into her white sweater even more.

I quit watching and started to write down my initial observations.

- *Taste and attraction varies*
- *What one person likes might repel someone else.*
- *Girls, especially, seem to know (or learn) how to catch the attention of guys they're interested in.*
- *Attraction has degrees; some guys notice but don't act, some notice and act, and some don't notice at all.*

At that moment, I looked up and saw several other girls sitting around the Shoppe. Some were together and some were alone. I saw one girl in particular who was hidden away looking at a book. She was attractive, but wore no makeup or earrings. She was lightly pulling on her long black hair, almost twisting it at the very end as she stroked it. What caught my eye was how she would dart her eyes up and off to the side. She kept this pattern up: looking at her book, twirling her hair, and darting her eyes. Suddenly I traced her glance.

She was looking at the two engineers in the back of the Shoppe! Quickly I added one more observation.

· Attraction apparently happens to everyone!

Just then Jake interrupted my note-taking. "More café, Annie?"

"No, thanks," I said. "I'm about to head out."

"I'm just getting off work; can I give you a lift?" Jake asked.

"Thanks, but I think I'll walk," I said.

"Your choice," he said smiling.

"The coffee's on me," he continued as he took off his Polmier's apron.

"Thanks, Jake," I said as I started to leave.

"Annie," he called out. "You forgot your jacket."

"Silly me," I said. "Silly, silly me," I said all the way back to my apartment.

My weekly call to Krista started as a chore, but as I began to practice what Glaen was helping me learn about observing, I began to look forward to it.

"So, how is Mike these days?" I had learned we were going to talk about Mike every time so I decided to bring him up myself.

"We broke up," Krista replied matter-of-factly.

"What happened doesn't he like you any more?"

"He still likes me, all my friends say so," she said.

After pulling a few teeth, I learned that Mike had somehow offended Krista's friends, so his punishment was for Krista to break up and not "like him" anymore. Actually, there was even more.

"Sis, do you and your friends 'trash' Mike for fun or are you just mad?"

"We're a lot nicer to Mike than most girls would be, believe me," she replied.

Wow! I wondered how many guys know the girls around them are dissecting them like frogs in a biology lab, with about the same results. I told Krista that it all sounded a little weird to me, but that I was still learning to observe. Finally, she gave me the résumé of her newest guy-target and our call ended.

I made a fresh entry in my notebook:

Although Krista never tires of talking about relationships with boys, she doesn't seem to know much about what one really is. However, I guess she is confident she knows all about them because she focuses so much attention on the subject. It's a pattern.

Now I'm pretty sure what they mean when they say a boy 'likes' them or that they 'like' a boy.

They make a trade. The guy puts his focus on the girl, and she gives affection to the guy. It's almost like an addiction, where each one wants more and more affection/attention until one or the other decides they've had enough or can't get enough. At the same time, the girl critiques the boyfriend, while the boy boasts of his conquest (real or imagined). In either case, they really aren't being themselves...and teens are the one's who say, "Get real!" I doubt Krista is ready to see any of this yet. Definitions may end conflicts, but that doesn't mean coming to agreement on them is easy!

"Well Annie, I'm quite proud of how well you've learned to observe. How's your faith?" Glaen said, after reviewing my notes.

"My faith is wonderful!" I blurted out. "Glaen, I've spent years saying that my relationship with God was good. I'm sure I believed in Christ at an early age, too. But honestly, I never knew a relationship with God could be so wonderful."

"How so?" Glaen asked.

"Well, I think...it's sort of like this." I took a breath and started again. "I was clearly taught that Jesus took away the guilt of all of my sins when I believed in Him and His death, burial, and resurrection. Oddly enough, though, I never felt fully convinced He really accepts me until I started making sense of faith. I kept trying to find some visible evidence or feeling that proved I am eternally OK. I finally realized that faith was really about accepting what He said to be true. You might say I have finally taken Him at His Word. The verse you gave me to reflect on made a big difference."

"How so, Annie?"

"Well, Hebrews 11:6 says we must believe that He 'is.' I decided that that must mean I need to believe what He tells me about Himself, so now the focus is on Him rather than on me.

Honestly, I think I was creating doubt by trying so hard to believe, and trying so hard to find proof. It was like I had my faith in everything I was doing, rather than in Christ where the focus belongs."

Glaen just looked at me with a curious smile.

"So, I think that when I was plagued with doubt, what I was really trusting was my sincerity in asking, or how I seemed to be living...anything other than what Jesus tells me to trust in; Him!"

"That's terrific Annie. What about the rest of the verse, did you reflect on that also?"

"Well some. I'm not sure I have much of that figured out yet. But, I guess that at least part of pleasing God is that we should care more about what He has promised to give us than what we can get from other places."

"That's a good start, Annie. A lot of folks much older than you have never been able to observe how much of their life is spent seeking rewards in the form of approval from other people rather than from their Creator. What difference is it making for you?"

"Well, the next thing I knew, what Jesus says in John 3:16 came alive for me. I have everlasting life because of *Him* and what *He* did. He said that if I believed in Him I would have everlasting life. I knew I believed, so all that was left was to thank Him!

As I kept thanking Him for His promise to me I became overwhelmed with a kind of knowing that didn't keep having to have proof. I knew because He had said it. When I focus on believing *Christ* and what *He* has promised, it seems my doubts vanish. Maybe I'll doubt again someday, but right now as I look at Him instead of myself, I'm at peace."

Glaen smiled and said, "Good, Annie. You have faith and the skill of observation. You are ready for your book. All you have to do is discover it."

"Discover it?" I said.

"Annie," Glaen said. "I know something you don't know. I know you have a book about relationships in your future. You just need to discover it."

I'm sure I frowned because Glaen kept explaining it to me.

"Do you remember when you got to advanced math in High School? Well, it's very similar. The trick to solving a mathematical problem is really just to keep working at it…and to keep making observations about the problem. Annie, here's the key to working on a problem: **Assume the answer pre-exists.**"

Glaen wrote those words on the board and continued. "If the answer pre-exists, then all you have to do is work until you find it. Do you believe God designed relationships to work? Of course you do, so Annie, the answer really does exist…even before you find it."

"So where do I start?" I asked.

"What are you trying to discover?" Glaen asked in return.

"I want to know the truth about how relationships work. And I think my faith is ready, faith that God designed them to work, and the truth is already there to be discovered," I stated with determination.

"Then what's always in the way of the truth?" Glaen added.

After I thought for a moment I answered. "Lies, I guess."

Glaen smiled and packed his satchel. "See you soon," he said.

So, as Glaen showed me, I began with lies. Here's what I discovered:

Lie #1

There's no harm in acting married; it's just practice.

Jennah helped me see this first lie. She, and most others, seem to think of dating as sort of being married. So, it makes sense to refer to a former boyfriend as an "EX" and as dating someone else on the sly as "cheating." In fact, when you make dating equal marriage, then "breaking up" is similar to a divorce. The result? Pain, heartache, and devastation. Pretending you're married also presumes a commitment which really isn't there; which in turn invites jealousy and possessiveness. Oddly, others don't see "dating" as being married, so it's open season on stealing someone away...after all, they're only "dating." Among Christians it has the added problem of tempting couples to start acting out roles about leading and following (another book?), rather than operating with respectful freedom toward each other. The countering truth is pretty simple:
You are ONLY married when you're married!

SUMMARY

<u>Lie #1</u>

There's no harm in acting married; it's just practice.

<u>Countering Truth</u>

You are ONLY married when you're married!

"Hello?" I said as the phone interrupted my writing.

"Annie, it's Dad."

"Hi Daddy, how are you?"

"I suppose I'm OK, Sweetheart, how's school?" he said.

"School's fine. I'm really enjoying this new professor. He's kinda weird, but after I'm through talking to him, I feel like I've learned the wisdom of the ages. What's up with you?" I said.

"Oh, not much…trying to stay busy and not think too much."

"You miss Mom?" I asked.

"Yes, I'm afraid I do. It's even worse when you live in a town like ours. Everyone wants to help, so they give me reports and sightings of your Mom's latest meanderings," he said as his voice trailed off at the end.

"So Mom's meandering…what are you doing?"

"Well," he said. "I'm not meandering, that's for sure." After a little silence, Dad went on– "You know Annie, I tried my best. I focused on your Mom all I could. I read books and they all said to be sensitive and romantic. I tried to be sensitive, and I think I was pretty good at that part. I listened. I let her complain. I even gave her the leeway to go pursue the things she wanted to do without me. I was patient, I was kind…."

"Dad," I interrupted. "You sound like you were a boy scou

"Well, I don't mean to imply that," he said. "I guess I failed
the romance part."

"What do you mean?" I asked, not really knowing what he
was thinking about.

"Well, you know when I took your mother up to Lake
Gauthier for the weekend?"

"Yes sir."

"I had paid an attendant at the resort to fill the room with
candles while we went on a walk. I also had ordered a tray of
strawberries injected with liquor and dipped in chocolate."

"Dad, you don't drink," I interrupted.

"Honey, they weren't for me," he answered with a wink in his
voice. "It's more of a flavoring than alcohol, anyway."

"So what happened?"

"Well, your Mom picked up a couple of the strawberries,
looked around at the candle-lit cabin, and said, 'Well, I'm tired so
I'll see you in the morning.'"

"Dad, that's terrible!" I said.

"Terrible or not, I slept on the couch, watched a documen-
tary on Egyptian mummification, and got sick on strawberries."

t. "

at

could feel something welling up inside.

angry...was she like that when you

ought a lot about that very thing; and don't be

the one that's changed. You know, as the years

your Mom slipping away from me. You got older

less of your mother's attention. She became interest-

ngs away from our family, and I felt she needed more

on."

"It sounds like you were at least trying," I interrupted.

"Well, maybe I was trying, but mostly I felt scared," he said. "I kept trying to be what I thought she wanted, and do what I thought she'd like; but somewhere in there, I lost me."

"You lost you?" I asked.

"Annie, I think your mother liked me more back when I was hard at work in law school and debated every point...just for practice. It wasn't that we argued, it was more that we shared our opinions openly. We agreed a lot, and stood firm on our own convictions. Those were great years. She was like a partner."

"Dad," I said a little cautiously. "Mom isn't remarried. I keep hoping you guys will get back together. Glaen, my writing professor, has had me thinking a lot about faith lately."

"Sweetheart," Dad interrupted. "Maybe we will, and may
we won't. I suspect even your professor would admit that none
us know the future. I can tell you, though; I'm really not intere
ed in making getting back with your mother a priority."

"Dad!" I cried out.

"I'm sorry Annie, but I've got someone much more important to win back than your mother," he said.

"Who's that?" I asked.

"Sweetheart, I've got to win myself back. As I think about it,
I lived a pretty big lie just to trying to please your Mom. I
really wasn't being myself."

"Dad, that doesn't excuse her behavior."

"You are probably right, but Honey that is her issue not
mine. What I know is that I suddenly feel focused. And I am
going to learn to be true to myself again! But, thank you, dear.
Your concern is a real encouragement."

"Great Dad," I said with sarcasm.

"Hey, Annie, keep writing," he said as we swapped our good-byes.

"I will, Daddy, I will…," I thought as I looked at my journal,
now stained with a new tear or two.

be
of
st-
, and only one, person for you
nd you will only find happiness
id that person.

't find any place where the Bible
ts for us to get all our fulfillment
one other person. Glaen made a passing
nment about "eternal life" in John 17:3 that
tarted me thinking. The verse says eternal life
is to know God and Jesus Christ. That seems
to be where satisfaction lies. I learned that
Romans 8:28 tells us that "God causes
all things to work together for good" for
believers, but then I saw that the next verse
defines what is "good;" that we become like
Christ. That has to mean that no matter what
circumstance we find ourselves in, God is
leading and working if we will listen, if we
will...believe!

There are plenty of cause-and-effect
verses; if we make bad choices we suffer the
consequences, so this obviously doesn't mean
I should be foolish in my choices...inviting a
lot of unnecessary suffering.

*Now as to marrying the right person,
1 Corinthians 7:39 says a widow can marry
whom she wishes as long as it's another
believer (" in the Lord," it says). So God's
focus must not be so much on " who we
marry" but on whether we will walk by faith
in the marriage.*

Countering Truth:
*God allows freedom inside the boundary
of marrying someone " in the Lord;" and,
happiness is something you build with the
Lord—not demand from your spouse.*

As I was about to write Lie #3, a lightning thought struck my
mind. I bet my mouth dropped open and my eyes bugged out.
Dad and Krista were twins! Dad was pretending to be someone
else to try to please Mom, and Krista was confessing all the
things she tries to get guys to like her. In each case they are basically trying to manipulate other people rather than relating to
them. If "truth is the lifeblood of relationships" as Glaen quoted,
then no wonder the relationships I'm observing are dead or
dying. I'm sure they mean well, but it's getting clear that their
methods won't get them what they want.

I wrote the next lie.

<u>Lie #3</u>

If you will follow the right process, you will be guaranteed a good marriage.

I started with the theory that if I could find the right process, I could learn how relationships work. But now I see it isn't a formula that makes the real difference.

No wonder I lost hope for the "courting" approach. Ken and Bette were just trying to do things perfectly so they could guarantee a good marriage. They had such a cool plan, I was thinking it was fail-safe. Now it is clear that relating is more than a set of steps you can learn from a book or a class.

I also think there is a trap in trying to guarantee how a relationship will go. It tempts people not to live in the present where relating really happens. Guaranteeing how a relationship will turn out is about the future; so in the midst of planning (and maybe scheming?) they miss out on really

connecting. Watching married couples, like
Trent & Deidre McNelson (my parents' friends)
shows that married couples do this very thing
as well. They worked so hard to save their
money and plan for trips and joys after they
RETIRED...unfortunately, between Trent's
heart problem and the collapse of their stocks,
they can't really enjoy the retirement they
wanted...and now they miss all those years of
working [this isn't just an observation, they
told me their story when I was home for
Christmas].

<u>Countering Truth:</u>
No process can guarantee a good
relationship, because there are no future
guarantees in relationships. Relationships
happen in the present.

Note: Include in the book... We don't know the future.

As I wrote the last line, the phone rang. It was Jake.

"Hi Annie, I've been thinking about something you said to me, and wanted to make a comment–if that's ok?"

"Sure, Jake," I replied. "Your comments are usually helpful; I would love to hear it. What did I say?"

"Well, you remember talking about what you could do to get your folks back together again...do you still want to hear my thought?"

Suddenly my throat tightened. "Sure," I heard myself say, even though I really wanted to change the subject. At least I was making a step toward maturity; I was hoping that by holding the tension I might discover something and grow a little.

"Well Annie, I went through this with a friend of mine. I could tell you the whole story, but the conclusion is that my friend made himself miserable trying to change something he really couldn't, instead of, you know..."

"Just trying live in the present?" I reluctantly added.

"Well yeah, that's a great way to put it, to live in the present."

"You might not believe this Jake, but I was just writing those words in my journal, but...," I stopped myself.

"But what Annie?"

"But I hadn't thought about this with my parents," I said.

"I guess this relationship thing is going to affect my life in ways I didn't expect," I whispered to myself.

Jake went on, "Well, I just felt like I needed to call and offer my experience, Annie. I'm glad you didn't think I was sticking my nose where it didn't belong." After a few polite words, I hung up with Jake, and looked back at my journal.

> When someone accepts the fact that she cannot know the future, then a new kind of power or opportunity comes into her life. She can quit trying to force and manipulate the future. She can quit trying to control her relationships. In fact, she should finally be able to start enjoying the relationship once she gives up on trying to guarantee its future.

SUMMARY

Lie #2

God has one, and only one, person for you to marry; and you will only find happiness if you find that person.

Countering Truth

God allows freedom inside the boundary of marrying someone "in the Lord;" and, happiness is something you build with the Lord—not demand from your spouse.

SUMMARY

<u>Lie #3</u>

If you will follow the right process, you will be guaranteed a good marriage.

<u>Countering Truth</u>

No process can guarantee a good relationship, because there are no future guarantees in relationships. Relationships happen in the present.

Lie #4
  Sex is...

Before I could finish writing the lie I had discovered about sex, Jennah came to mind. Earlier in the day we had met and talked through the whole idea about trying to guarantee everything.

"But I want to make sure my next one really works," she said.

"I think that's what we're talking about," I replied.

"I don't understand. How can admitting I can't make a relationship work help me make sure a relationship will work?" she asked a little frustrated about the whole topic.

"Jennah, tell me your story about guys again."

"OK…I meet a guy. He's interested and I'm interested. He likes me and I like him. After a while he starts neglecting me and I get mad. Then he gets nicer…," she stopped in mid-sentence.

"And?" I said.

"And, he neglects me again and I get really mad…."

"Until it's over, right?" I asked.

"But it's not my fault," she interrupted. "They're just selfish. All I'm trying to do is make sure we spend time together and get to know each other."

"Why are you trying to make sure?" I asked.

"Well, I just don't want it to end like the last time."

"Jenn, don't you see? Trying to 'make sure' is the same as trying to guarantee it will all work out the way you want it to. Here's an example," I said. "Do you remember when you took care of Libby's wedding reception last June?"

"Sure," she smiled.

"What did you do with the caterers?"

"I stayed on them and made sure they did everything they had agreed to do," she said.

"Right. And why did you stay on them?" I asked.

"You know, Annie. Libby was so distracted with the baby on the way and her Mom's lack of involvement; well, I just wanted to make sure the reception was wonderful."

"Yeah, and what did the caterer tell us later?" I said while I patted her hand.

Jennah looked down and smiled. "I get it."

"You get what?" I asked.

"That caterer said she'd never do another event I was involved with," Jennah said almost too quiet to hear.

"I know you were trying to make sure that things were perfect, but it made you…."

"Controlling," she said.

"Yes! Jenn, you are a really good person; but you were sort of up to no good. You were forcing them to do everything your way." I said.

"I know, but they were being paid."

"Good point. Actually, I'd never hire them again either…she definitely had issues," I added. We both laughed.

"I think it just comes down to a really old fashioned truth we've heard since we were little girls: The Golden Rule," I said.

"You mean the, 'Do unto others…' rule?" she asked.

"The same," I nodded.

"So, I should treat guys how I'd like to be treated…like with patience, and kindness, and honesty…and, even be understanding?" Jennah said dramatically.

"It sort of ruins the idea of being a 'princess,' doesn't it?" I said.

"Gee, thanks," Jennah said. "But, you're still my friend," she added with a smile.

I went back to my journal.

> I guess being truthful in relationships without the Golden Rule might be pretty harsh. I don't really want to say everything to someone else that I think is true, but I do want to say those things I would want them to tell me; things I need to hear for my own good to make better choices. Now,
>
> Lie #4
> Sex is something special God wants committed people to enjoy.
>
> The sex lie is perhaps the most dangerous because, in a sense, it's true! Sex actually is something special that God wants us to enjoy, and the enjoyment is intended for a committed relationship. But this type of commitment can not occur outside of marriage. Well, I guess

it can. I know we Christians tend to force our values on others. But, you cannot be more-or-less committed. We are either committed, or we are not.

Personally, I think the Bible is right when it leaves no room for sex outside of marriage. Marriage is about as clear a commitment as you can have-still without a guarantee of the future. So that means in dating relation ships sex can really distort true relating to another person. In fact, a lot of guys and girls think love and relationship is a gradual progression toward a commitment, and that gradual progression includes a gradual progression towards sex. But as the Bible predicts, instead of being special, it gets elevated to an appetite, like being hungry or thirsty. At that point sex becomes the point of the relationship, and relating is getting its last rites.

I guess that's what's behind what the speaker said a few weeks ago at H.O.W., " Girls tend to give sex to get love...and...Guys tend to give love to get sex." I know it's an overstatement, but it is pretty observable. And it leads to an ugly picture.

I probably should ask everyone who reads the book, " How many other girls would you like your husband to have slept with before you?" Or, " How many other guys would you like your wife to have slept with before you?" Isn't " none" a most excellent answer?

Countering Truth

When sex is common, it isn't special. Sex is something special God wants married people to enjoy.

Of course, since dating, courting, and engagement aren't marriage, sex is reserved for the honeymoon. Thinking about it, doesn't that help make the honeymoon special...when you are together for the first time?

SUMMARY

<u>Lie #4</u>

Sex is something special God wants committed people to enjoy.

<u>Countering Truth</u>

When sex is common, it isn't special. Sex is something special God wants married people to enjoy.

The more you look, the more you see.
Just see the obvious.

It became my habit. I went to Polmier's to observe. I wrote
these two sentences at the top of my journal every time I made
observations. They were from Glaen's pen and mouth, and they
were important. By now I had pages of things I had noticed
about relationships, but today something new was becoming
obvious to me about guys and girls.

"Another latte, Annie?" Jake asked.

"Sure, I'm here for a while."

"How's the project coming? Got relationships solved yet?"

"Well, to tell you the truth, I've come a long way. But the
fact is that I've got one little piece that's a complete mystery to
me," I told Jake.

"Let me get your latte and this customer who just walked in,
then I'd love to hear it," Jake said as he hurried to the counter.

"I wish I knew how to think about it. It seems to be universal, and especially with girls. I have pored over my notes and one thing keeps coming back up. In all my interviews I see nothing but conflict coming out of this one assumption. I wish I could put my finger on it. Maybe Jake has an idea," I thought as I sat there and reviewed my journal. Soon he came back.

"One latte, the cinnamon's free," Jake kidded since I hate cinnamon in my latte.

"So what's on your mind?" he asked.

"Well, it's romance."

"You getting too much or too little?" he joked.

Ignoring him, I answered, "Jake, with all the people I've interviewed, I keep finding that a lack, or maybe over-expectation, of romance keeps hurting relationships."

"Girls seem to think it's really important," he observed.

"Yes they do. But there's nothing but conflict that finally comes out of it. The only exceptions are with couples who seem to be 'romantic' only on occasion. It's true in the marriages I've interviewed, as well. What's the deal with romance?"

"Do you like it?" he asked.

"Hmm...well, I...."

"Oops…Annie, I've got to run. Class just let out, and here comes the 'Principles of Investing' crowd. Oh, and there's Jennah anyway. Let's finish this later." Jake said as he got up from the table.

"Hi Annie," Jennah looked brighter than I ever remembered.

"What's up?" I asked.

"Well, first I want to give you this little gift," she said as she handed me a small white box, gift wrapped from James Avery.

"What's it for?" I asked.

"It's a 'thank you.'"

I opened the box to find a beautiful polished lapel pin of an Angel.

"Thanks Jennah, but what did I do?" I asked as I put it on immediately.

"You've been an Angel to me! I can't tell you what a difference learning about relationships has meant to my life," she said.

"Oh, you're just in love again, since Jake introduced you to Steve," I smiled back.

"Well, maybe I am in love; but it's the first time I feel relaxed about just having a relationship. I didn't realize what a burden I put on guys by assuming we were kind of married when we were dating," Jennah said as she smiled, looked down, and shook her head.

"What?" I asked.

"Well, I was just thinking how much time I lost and how much pain I caused by trying to make guys look at me and treat me the way I wanted to be treated," she said. "I really was just trying to be a princess; trying to control them and guarantee the relationship would go the way I wanted it to."

"Well, you know…   "

"I know," Jennah interrupted. "I know that relationships occur in the present, like you showed me. I know that the past is over, too. I just wish I had known sooner so I could have enjoyed just letting guys be themselves instead of the kind of 'husband' or 'boyfriend' they should be for me. I'll give you an example. Yesterday, Steve told me he was going hunting for the weekend with his guys' Bible study group. I felt fine. I could even cheer for him and hope he has a great time. Annie, in the past I would have been hopping mad because I would have thought he should spend all his spare time with me; and for sure, at least ask for my permission to go hunting. It isn't just that I used to think we were sort of 'married', I thought we were chained to each other! Now the 'do unto others' Rule really is Golden to me."

"You know what confuses me?" I asked. Jennah didn't answer, but just looked at me with her settled brown eyes.

"Not, why didn't we know sooner; but why God would let us see this now instead of when we're fifty?" We both laughed.

"I know you're right, Annie," Jennah said. "I'm glad I know it now even if it would have been nice to have known it sooner."

"Thanks for the pin," I said.

"Thanks for the help and friendship," she replied.

We sat in the coffee Shoppe for a long quiet moment together. The normal crowd kept moving through Polmier's. Basically, only four kinds of groups come to the Shoppe. Singles, groups of girls, groups of guys, and couples. The couples were the ones I was taking notes on that day.

"So, what are you learning today?" Jennah asked.

"Well, I think I'm seeing another lie."

Just then Jake walked up. "Hi ladies," he said. "As two of our most faithful patrons, I want to offer you the first sampling of our new Raspberry Crumble Cream Cake. In keeping with the academic motif, we simply call it RC3. One slice, two forks, no objections," Jake concluded with a wink and walked back to the counter.

"You know, Annie…," Jennah said.

"I know, Jennah. I just am not ready," I said.

"He obviously likes you. What's to get ready for? It's not like you'd have to act married if you got together." Jennah enjoyed jabbing me a little too much.

"OK, I'll pray about it. Now can I tell you what I'm learning?" I said without waiting for an answer.

"Here we have a fork and a spoon. What makes one a fork and one a spoon?" I asked.

"Hmm," Jennah said. "This isn't one of those 'the-sound-of-one-hand-clapping' kind of questions, is it?"

"No. Just look for the most obvious thing."

"Well," she began. "A fork has four pointy things while a spoon is more like a little bowl on a handle."

"Nice," I said. "And that is exactly the point. It is the distinctions or differences that define each. They each have handles, are made from the same kind of metal, are used to eat with, etc. But what makes a spoon a spoon, and a fork a fork, is how they differ."

"OK, so what does this have to do with relationships?" Jennah asked.

"Well, Jennah, it's pretty clear. You and I live in a time when it seems our teachers and the media keep telling us, as women, that we can do anything a man can do. Never mind that I can also do anything a dog can do...."

"Annie, did you just call guys 'dogs'?" Jennah interrupted.

We both broke out in laughter and the whole Shoppe stopped moving to look at us.

"Shhh...No, guys aren't dogs, well not all of them," I said as we laughed again.

"What I mean is that everyone keeps insisting that guys and girls are the same. I know we have a lot of similarities; but it's the differences that define men and women. Here's how I've written it:

Lie #5
    Men and women are basically the same.

Countering Truth
    The differences, not the similarities, define women and men.

"So what?" Jennah asked.

"Jennah, it affects everything! If we can start to understand the differences between guys and girls, we can start cheering for everyone to celebrate their unique design. Guys could act like they were designed to act. Girls could do the same. There wouldn't be pretense or a campaign for everyone to be the same. We could go ahead and be feminine and they could be masculine. The way it is now, most of us feel like we have to be more competitive to be a true 'woman.' All the guys have to be softer and yielding. It's like they are supposed to be like us and we are supposed to be like them."

"So, they ARE dogs!" Jennah blurted out. "And we're cats!" This time our laughter got a cold stare from the girl studying Russian alone at the back table.

"I'm not saying I understand all the differences, I'm just saying the distinctions really clarify a lot about our approach to things, our roles in the relationship, our responses to each other. Guys are different, and so are we. The more we try to deny or change this fact, the further away from real relationships we travel."

"Ladies," Jake interrupted. "Do I need to muzzle either of you?"

"No, Jake," I said. "Just get us a litter box or put us outside, we'll be fine." We giggled like a couple of girls as we left Polmier's. And, on impulse, I turned and winked at Jake on the way out.

SUMMARY

<u>Lie #5</u>

Men and women are basically the same.

<u>Countering Truth</u>

The differences, not the similarities, define women and men.

"Well, here's my journal. And here are the lies I've collected so far," I told Glaen as I walked into the classroom. Glaen carefully worked through my notes page after page, occasionally smiling and occasionally murmuring. He was such a curious man to me, no mention of a life outside of this classroom, but a deep confidence that he was doing just what he wanted to in life. I wanted that too, and I wanted someone like Glaen to marry.

"Annie? Annie?" Glaen startled me from my thoughts.

"Sorry, I was thinking," I said.

"Thinking is good," Glaen smiled to me.

"Annie, what is a relationship? I see you keep focusing on the topic, but I don't see a definition."

"Well, let's see," I said.

"The dictionary talks about connection and association, but I think we mean something more. I know it is a connection between at least two things," I said as a thumbed through my notes. "Here it is…a connection between at least two people."

"So what is going on with this connection?" Glaen asked.

"I think maybe influence is the answer. Not the influence of control or force, but the influence that naturally happens when two objects connect, like in physics," I offered.

"Influence?" Glaen asked.

"Glaen, it's like the earth and the moon. The earth has a big influence on the moon, since it keeps it in orbit. But the moon has an influence on the earth, as in the tides of the oceans," I said.

"So, in relationships people are connected in a way that influences one another," Glaen prodded.

"Yes...but it's not like trying to control someone...it's like the nature of things; you know, how God set things up."

"Bad company," Glaen nodded.

"That's random. What do you mean?" I asked.

"Annie, in your Bible there is a verse that states, 'Bad company corrupts good morals...'"

"Oh yeah! Two weeks ago a speaker at church was talking about that in 1 Corinthians 15...how did he say it? *You'll never be like the people you don't hang around.*' I guess that means we might want to be picky about our friends and our future partners. If we all have some influence on one another, being around people who are good for you is probably a smart move," I added.

"Good," Glaen said. "Now tell me what you are currently observing about relationships."

My mind raced because the implications about friendships were a little staggering. Most of us don't give much consideration to who we should befriend, but the nature of relationships suggests that we are wiser when we connect with people who are good for us…and people we are good for, as well. Suddenly I realized this conversation matched my next four insights.

"OK Glaen, here you go," I said. "There are four words to summarize my recent observations; Love, Chemistry, Basis, and Lust. The principles look like this:

1. *Love is a mystery of choices*
2. *Chemistry in relationships is God's business*
3. *The Basis for relationships is our business*
4. *Lust is an appetite which owns its possessor*

"Interesting, Annie. What do they mean?" Glaen asked.

"Well, let me explain them one-at-a-time. ***Love is a mystery of choices*** means that no one knows everything about how love really works, but God tells us it is mainly about choices we are to take, by faith, without thinking about the reactions of others. As I've made observations and interviewed people, it seems universal that people think that love sort of 'happens.' They usually use the term 'fall in love,' implying that love is something accidental or suddenly surprising. As I've made observations and interviewed people, it seems universally believed that love sort of 'happens.' I guess you could say most people see themselves as 'victimized' by love. But Glaen, no one so far in my research really 'falls in love' at first sight; there is more to it than that. We are attracted, sometimes at first sight; but other times, attraction surprises us with someone we've known for a long time. It seems that we can't choose to romantically love just anyone, but we also don't HAVE TO fall in love with a particular person. When people 'fall in love' it is an interaction in the relationship…like they both help move each other toward love…never on purpose like trickery, but subtly like the earth and the moon.

One person makes a choice and acts, then the other makes a choice and responds. The response is an action too, so the first person makes a new choice and counteracts. This cycle keeps happening until either love blossoms, or at least one of the two quits. Glaen, it's like this: A guy meets a girl he is interested in and smiles. She smiles back. He says something, often stupid, and she responds kindly. He winks, she winks. He asks her to lunch, she accepts. She gives him a token of friendship, he offers a token of fondness…Well you get the idea. If one or the other quits responding or can't respond, then this **mysterious dance** of choices is stopped in its tracks. But, something in all of this began to bother me. 1 Corinthians 13 says that love is a set of actions we take toward others with their best interest in mind – doing it God's way. Now, I know that I'm studying 'romantic love,' but why should it be off the hook with God? It seems that when we do love God's way, romantically or not, each person is serving the best interest of the other. In a still mysterious dance, the relationship grows as each responds by being more concerned about the other person. It isn't control…it's…love, I guess. It's sort of counter-intuitive; when we try to control the other person and 'make them love us,' then love really can't bloom at all."

"What about those who try to approach love apart from God's way?" Glaen asked.

"I think that has a lot to do with the second point about chemistry. **'Chemistry in relationships is God's business.'** We all know that people can have 'chemistry' between themselves. I guess this became a cliché because it matches how chemicals interact. If you put together certain chemicals they make medicine, but other chemicals when mixed, make poison."

"Or, they can cause an explosion," Glaen added.

"Well said," I mumbled as I wrote "explosion" in my journal.

"Anyway," I continued. "Some chemicals work well together, and some don't. It's the same with people, some people work well together and others don't. Basically this is the idea behind being attracted to someone. Honestly, Glaen, it seems people just 'like who they like and don't like who they don't like.' There are all kinds of wild theories about this simple fact. When it is about relationships, the basic beginning point is often just this attraction."

"Are you saying attraction is just about chemicals?" Glaen asked.

"No, not JUST chemicals," I told him abruptly. "It's also about how two people fit together. A guy and a girl who have good chemistry just fit well together, and everyone seems to know it. Their demeanor and actions match. The way they walk, talk, and look at each other also seems like it was planned before time. I guess in today's lingo we'd say when there isn't chemistry, 'He doesn't do it for me.' It's so intangible that we just label it, 'It.' Proverbs 30:18-19 tells us, 'There are three things which are too wonderful for me, four which I do not understand... Number four on the list is 'the way of a man with a young woman.' Glaen, this cloaked interaction of chemistry is a very frustrating part of working on this book; it just isn't predictable."

"True, but it does make things interesting...," Glaen mused. "So, why do you say it's God's business?"

"Well, I think it's like the chemicals," I said with a little confidence. "God designed the chemicals and how they interact when put together. We don't really know why they react to each other the way they do, but we do know God made them that way. It seems much the same with people. Truly mysterious things in the design of God's creation are best left to Him. That's why I refer to it as God's business. I think it's best to leave it in the hands of God, and take chemistry between people the way God made it."

"So, your attraction and match with another person could be a big hint from God?" Glaen asked.

"Big HINT from God," I wrote in my journal just below the words *Chemistry in relationships is God's business*.

I told Glaen, "Well put, again."

"What about couples who are already married, or who are already committed to each other? What if they don't have good chemistry?" Glaen asked.

"I haven't investigated that much," I said. "But thinking out loud, they could call it off…that seems to be what is happening a lot." My mind wandered to my parents for a moment. "And it's probably smart for unmarried couples who aren't a match to call it off, like my Theory 2 friends. On the other hand, many couples seem to make the Basis of the relationship enough." That's what I wish my parents would do, I thought to myself.

"Have you thought about a catalyst?" Glaen asked.

"You mean like in chemistry?" I said.

"I thought you said this WAS chemistry," Glaen winked at me.

"Look up catalyst and how it affects a chemical reaction," I mumbled as I wrote in my journal again.

"Glaen," I said. "I know people can pray for God to change their hearts; that must be one catalyst. However, this sounds a lot like romance. And I can't find where romance as a goal has a long-term helpful affect on relationships. It seems like everyone starts lusting for romantic experiences instead of growing real relationships.

Maybe there is a catalyst, but if it is romance it only seems to hurt. I just don't understand why?"

"Hmm...." Glaen looked down and stroked his fine white beard. "Annie, I know someone who has thought about this exact issue. I'm going to find her book and bring it to you at our next class."

"Wow, thanks if it'll help," I said.

"I think you'll like what she has to say. How about explaining what you mean by Basis," Glaen added.

"Okay, like I said, **'The Basis for relationships is our business.'** Basis is really about the foundation of the relationship. When two people are in a relationship, especially looking toward marriage, they are really talking about a commitment to build a life together as partners. The basis is about whether or not there is a good foundation for the long-term relationship. If there is a bad foundation, then the relationship will likely crumble over time."

"Give me an example," Glaen asked.

"Well," I began. "One couple I interviewed really seemed to be in love and had dated for about two years. When it got down to marriage, however, they were in a real conflict. As I kept up with their story, it turned out that she, Gwen, was so committed to being near her mother and father that she insisted he, Thomas, pursue a career in her hometown. Thomas was finishing his law degree and was fixed on practicing law as an entrance into running for public office. Gwen's home is a small town in Missouri. Thomas explained to Gwen that there weren't many jobs available for new lawyers in the town, and that if he got elected, they'd eventually have to move anyway."

"So what happened?" Glaen interrupted.

"They broke up. Gwen moved back to her hometown and is a nurse at the hospital. Thomas took a job in Atlanta with a law firm which specializes in international law. It turned out that where to live was a **deal-killer** for their relationship. In the end they were both sad, but neither was angry. It became really clear that they both valued things that wouldn't really let them build a life together. They didn't have a good basis," I said.

"Sounds like deal-killers are important for unmarried couples to discover," Glaen observed. In that moment I felt a flooding thankfulness for Glaen. I hadn't often talked to a man who was so interested in what was interesting to me. I knew at that second in time I wanted a relationship with someone who had a shared love for the things that mattered most to me, who would support me in my pursuits; a true life partner. Right then I decided never to compromise my own *basis*.

"Deal-killers are the key," I said. "Since the principle is **'the Basis for relationships is our business,'** I've concluded that finding if there is a match is often a matter of discovering deal-killers. Asking, 'What things are so important to me that I will not compromise them?' is an example of a good way to find the deal-killers. **A deal-killer is a foundational issue on which neither person in a relationship will compromise.**

If building a life as a Christian couple is vital to a person, then marrying an atheist or a Muslim wouldn't really be a match. Moreover, it wouldn't be right to ask an atheist to give up his belief just for the sake of marriage."

"People might think you're quite politically incorrect," Glaen noted.

"I know, but they'd just be missing the point," I said. "It could be about anything, not just one's faith. What if one partner thought having affairs throughout a marriage was the way to go? It's not much of a match for a person committed to being involved with only one person."

"OK," Glaen said. "What about Basis being 'your' business?"

"I think it is a matter of one's choice and values," I said. "We don't really have much of a choice with chemistry, but when it comes to being true to our values and making a choice about what we want our life to grow toward...I think we are the ones to make the final decision here. It also looks pretty clear that God has left this to us as well; not that God doesn't give us pretty clear directions on some things."

"So Gwen could have decided to support Thomas, and just call her mother everyday from Atlanta?" Glaen asked.

"Exactly," I said. "Or she could decide to support Thomas and give him the freedom to pursue his dream, while keeping to her own value of building a life back home; which is just what she did."

"Annie, you're doing a great job. I see a real future for this book," Glaen said as he leaned back in his chair and put his hands behind his head.

"What about loving someone who doesn't love you back...I think they call that unrequited love," Glaen asked.

"Well, I could be wrong here, but that seems more like lust or appetite rather than real love. I'm not ruling out that someone could love a person who is not responding, that is actually what 1 Corinthians 13 tells us. Most people think of love as romance, in the Hollywood sense, which has more to do with our feelings.

But, romance does seem special and exciting. It's like most people are actually "in love" with the idea of "being in love." That kind of love seems to be about themselves and the way they feel, not about loving another person."

"Are you saying that it is wrong to have intense feelings, Annie?"

"Not at all. Intense feelings can be a great blessing, but they can also be a great distraction. If we seek feelings as our whole purpose, then we will have a problem because they change; and sadly, we get hooked on trying to recapture the feelings. That is what this last point is about."

"Well, tell me. I'm about out of time," Glaen said.

"Sure. My last point is that **Lust is an appetite which owns its possessor.** Lust is a desire that is more like a basic appetite or an appetite out of control. Desiring affection, or chocolate, or alcohol isn't necessarily wrong, but when it becomes the center of one's life, freedom is traded for slavery. A person who must have his desired object and spends all of his time pursuing it is a slave serving his master. Alcohol is pretty obvious because once a person becomes addicted to the drug, he is truly its slave.

"With girls and guys in dating type relationships, lust can take over in lots of forms. Obviously someone can desire another person's body to satisfy his craving; and this often goes with the guy. Someone else can desire the total attention of the other person, which is also lust; usually, I've noticed, this goes with us girls. Glaen, most of what's passed off as dating is really just a dance of cravings. A girl has an enslaving desire for attention and serves her master well to attract a guy. A guy has an enslaving desire for sex and serves his master well to coax a girl towards sex. I know there are other scenarios, but honestly, this is the one that seems to keep happening. Sadly, because they aren't really relating, they don't have much of a chance for a lasting relationship. Eventually, lust runs them to the next thing (or person) as the previous one just doesn't 'do it' for them anymore. Love satisfies, but lust it seems, never can."

"So what's the difference between lust and chemistry?" Glaen asked.

"You know Glaen, that's the problem. Most "lust" is just chemistry turned in on itself. I think the Hollywood myth we find in magazines, movies, and novels is all about chemistry being the beginning and end of all relationships…Hey, maybe that's why people think they "fall in love," it's just chemistry seeking its own interests."

"Maybe that's why human beings seem to "fall out of love" too." Glaen smiled.

"Glaen. That WOULD be it!" I screamed. "When lust is gone, then love is gone...so says Hollywood and the sillier side of fairytales." I paused and withdrew to myself for a moment, feeling I was losing something I had wanted deep within as a little girl, yet gaining something I now hoped for as a young woman.

"Annie, you are making great progress," Glaen snapped me back into the present moment. "See you next week with a surprise in hand," he said as he headed out the door.

"I still don't get romance," I murmured as I stashed my journal in my backpack. "I still don't get romance."

FOUR WORDS OF RELATIONSHIPS

1. <u>Love</u> is a mystery of choices.
2. <u>Chemistry</u> in relationships is God's business
   - Chemistry is the mutual attraction between two people.
   - Chemistry is often a Big Hint from God
3. The <u>Basis</u> for relationships is our business
   - Basis is about whether or not there is a good foundation to build a life together.
4. <u>Lust</u> is an appetite which owns its possessor
   *Hollywood's Myth: when you're out of lust you're out of love.

DEAL-KILLERS

A deal-killer is a foundational issue on which neither person in a relationship will compromise.

It was a long and uneventful walk back to my apartment. I thought about all I had learned about relationships. I thought about the fact that there are no guarantees, how love is about response and action, and about chemistry and the basis for relationships. I also kept thinking something was missing. No matter what, it was time to share something with my sister.

It seemed that since we are family it should be easier to approach Krista on a sensitive topic. Maybe, because we are family, it is harder. "Speaking the truth, the golden rule, definitions settle conflict," I rehearsed to myself, getting ready for what I had to share with Krista. Over the weeks the talks we had grew to be a joy as I practiced what I was learning. Between all the observing, which Krista saw as listening, our conversations were blooming into a real relationship!"

But as I paid attention, and because I loved her, I knew I needed to share a few of my concerns with her. "Lord, help me show Krista I care as I speak the truth," I muttered under my breath as I dialed her number.

After we caught up for a minute or two, I asked, "Krista, may I share a few things I've been learning? I think I'm seeing something that could help you a lot."

"Sure, I guess. Do you think I need help?" Krista said. I could tell the defense mechanisms were kicking in. I knew just how she felt; not knowing what's coming never feels good.

"Oh, I think we all need help. I hope you love me enough to share your insights with me too someday. I really want to just ask you a question," I said.

"Okay, fire away."

"Krista, if you could order a man directly from God for you, what would he be like?"

Well this part was easy. Her list was pretty long and pretty idealistic. The guy she described probably doesn't exist except in novels and dreams. He was to be powerful yet gentle, competitive yet understanding, sociable but a listener, etc.

"That's great Krista. I'd like this guy myself. But I have another question, 'If this guy existed, do you think he would keep his attention only on you?'" I asked.

"I don't get what you mean," she said.

"Well, a guy like that would have a lot he'd want to do in this world, and he'd want someone to do it with. But do you think he'd really keep his attention on you all the time?"

"Oh, I guess that would be kinda unfair," Krista admitted. "But I'm not doing that to my boyfriends."

I spent some time trying to help Krista see that her actions told a different story; her 'meanness', her shooing them away, and her being upset, all served to tell the guy that he "better keep his attention on Krista—or else!" Every step was manipulation; trying to control him, rather than relating with him. As Krista didn't really "get it" my frustration began to rise. I thought, "Maybe there's something else about relationships I don't understand." So, I decided to drop it for the time being.

"Krista, I think you have a lot on the ball, and I always enjoy talking to you. I'm sorry it took Mom and Dad splitting up to show me what a cool sister you are." At least I had learned that a genuine compliment is received well by everyone. Mostly, all I really knew at that moment was that I needed to stop and recharge.

"Yes, a large cheese-crust pepperoni pizza. No, no coupons. Thirty minutes is fine," I said as I hung up the phone. I decided a break was the right next step. "I'm going to eat a pizza, make a milkshake, and watch a mindless romantic comedy." My therapy was a lot cheaper than going to a counselor.

"Why do relationships go sour?" I asked myself, still feeling that thinning feeling in my heart when I thought about my mother and father. Their divorce was clean, and over two months earlier. Dad was broken and alone, while Mom was out dancing through the dating circles. I didn't want to take sides, but I felt like I was a judge in a talent show. Birthday, Christmas, phone calls...I got double presents and double attention. Dad wanted to talk about Mom, while Mom wanted to talk about the bachelor-de-jour.

"What goes wrong with relationships?" I thought as I made the first half of my milkshake before the pizza arrived. I learned during a stay in the hospital as a child that if you don't eat some dessert first, you may not have room to eat any later. Well, at that hospital the food wasn't good, but there was a lot of it.

"What goes wrong?" I asked again. I had interviewed so many people who shared the same story. The chemistry was great, the values were a match, but the relationship drifted into constant fighting. "Why do people fight?" I asked as I stabbed the shake with my favorite twirly-straw.

The silence floated in front of me as the frozen sweetness warmed my heart and soothed me for the moment. I picked up the remote and turned on the TV and the DVD player. I had picked up a movie called Roses, Dunces, and Don Juan, which is a comedy about two sisters who own a flower shop and give love lessons to guys who come to buy flowers for their moody girlfriends.

"No Signal" the television flashed at me. "No signal," I said, punching the "play" button on the remote. "No Signal" it flashed again. I punched it again, and again, but harder each time. Suddenly the DVD whirred and ejected the disk. I pushed the disk back in and stepped back to watch. "Playing" appeared on the screen in glowing green letters. I turned around and returned to the couch. As I sat, "No Signal" started flashing again. I hit the play button as hard as I could over and over again, but "No Signal" just kept mocking me. "I hate this machine," I said as I threw the remote down.

Just then someone knocked at the door, "Pizza Dude,"
he hollered.

"Just a minute," I yelled back as the DVD whirred again and
spit the movie at me. I couldn't help thinking it was sticking out
its tongue at me. "Why won't you do what I want you to?" I said
in disgust as I opened my apartment door.

A lanky guy with highlighted black hair and a nose ring
looked at me with surprise. "Hey," he said. "You sound just like
my girlfriend."

"Huh?" I said.

"Yeah…like she says, 'We never do what I want to do.'"

"Oh," I answered. "I was talking to my stupid DVD player."

"Cool." He smiled, "I thought you chicks were like in a con-
spiracy against me."

"We probably are," I said as I gave him a twenty dollar bill.
"What did you say to her?"

He looked at me with a wistful little grin and said, "I told
her that she was like totally right…because even when I do what
she wants, I don't do it the right way."

"What did she say back?" I asked.

"I don't know, I left with your pizza. She's like the manager or something. I feel like I'm a DVD she owns, but like I'm the totally wrong movie. You know, like when you get the right box with the wrong disk inside. I keep trying to be a stinkin' musical, but deep down I'm really a sci-fi thriller!"

"Keep the change," I said. "And keep telling the truth…it'll all work out for the best."

As I closed the door I got it.

Journal Entry

Tonight, in an incident with a remote
control and a pizza guy, I got the answer
to my questions, "Why do relationships
go bad?" and "Why do couples fight?"
It may not be the absolute answer, since
stress and hardships often contribute to
conflict. But as Newton showed the way
to observe and see principles, I think I
get it now.

It all comes down to four simple words:
Control
Truth
Love
Freedom

First, back to the remote control. Tonight I found myself screaming at my DVD player because it wouldn't do what I wanted. Isn't that what happens in relationships? Isn't a fight always about someone not doing what the other person wants? It may be that the person isn't saying the right words; or perhaps the words are right, but the way the words are said isn't. It could be about acting right or not acting wrong, how I'm treated, or how he should act. It doesn't really matter, because at the core of it all it is a dance of manipulation. Just agree with me and do what "I want," both could be saying at the same time.

One person wants the other person to act a certain way, usually to make her feel better. Next, the first person uses her behavior as a tool to get the other person to act "right." Think of any example. I remember Jennah telling me about Steve going hunting with the guys. In the past she would have pitched a fit because he wouldn't be with her that weekend. The goal of her fit would be to control, to make Steve cancel his plans and reorganize his life for her demands. In this case, if he didn't like her behavior (getting upset), then he could easily counter-act by getting really upset at her being upset. Amazingly, however, he could just as easily give in to stop her from being upset with him. In either of these situations, both of them are trying to control the other one. Jennah would be trying to control Steve by getting him not to go hunting. Steve would be trying to control Jennah by getting her to back off or shut up.

Robert Fritz adds something very helpful here he calls the "math of relationships." He observes that it takes two to say "yes" and one to say "no." If a guy invites a girl to dinner and she says, "Yes," then it is a yes. If she says, "No," then it is a no. The same turns out to be true about control or manipulation. It takes two people for a manipulation to happen. One has to try to control the other one, and the other has to play along. In either event, they aren't really relating because they're busy trying to control each other.

I could say it a little differently, "If I insist the other person acts or reacts a certain way toward me, then I am harming the possibility of relating by being controlling." Genuine relating happens when two people tell each other the truth. When we start trying to control the other person, then a manipulation is under way.

Manipulation means I'm not acting truthfully, and I'm not supporting the other person in being truthful. I'm using my actions to MAKE them act a certain way; and usually, they respond by using their actions to MAKE me act a certain way. Simply put:

Control means the other person isn't free to tell the truth...so he usually isn't his true and honest self (if he's playing along).

Truth means telling what you honestly think and acting as you really are. It's being true to yourself and how God has made you.

Love means acting with the Golden Rule in mind.

Freedom means it is important to you that the other person responds however he chooses to respond, even if you don't like it.

SUMMARY

Manipulation

Manipulation occurs when someone tries to control how another person thinks, feels, or acts.

Manipulation usually harms the possibility of relating by removing freedom.

Fritz's Math of Relationships

It takes two to say "yes" and one to say "no"; for every relationship decision, and especially, for any manipulation.

SUMMARY

<u>Control</u>

Control means the other person isn't free to tell the truth…so he usually isn't his true and honest self (if he's playing along).

<u>Truth</u>

Truth means telling what you honestly think and acting as you really are. It's being true to yourself and how God has made you.

<u>Love</u>

Love means acting with the Golden Rule in mind. (Golden Rule = do unto others as you would have them do unto you.)

<u>Freedom</u>

Freedom means it is important to you that the other person responds however he chooses to respond, even if you don't like it.

If this were written as math it would add up something like this:

Chemistry

+ Basis

+ Truth

+ Love

<u>+ Freedom (or minus Control)</u>

= Authentic Relating

I realized I had been talking too much.

"Jennah, I'm sorry, I know I've been talking non-stop the whole time. It's just that I'm so excited finally to see something special about how God designed relating to work. And, duh, love plays a bigger role than I imagined."

"It seems sort of complicated," Jennah mused, "but it also seems kind of simple."

"Jenn, I think it's hard because it's easy. Most of the guys and girls I've known have suffered from ignoring these principles. They think it can't be as simple as it seems," I replied.

"Or, they just didn't know them," Jennah corrected me.

"Good point," I said. "But, we girls in particular seem prone to desperately try to make the guys act how we want them to act...usually drippy-sweet and totally focused on us."

"Tell it all...I'm that woman," Jennah confessed like she was in a southern prayer meeting. "But it's not just the girls," she added.

"Right. Guys also want the girls to be how they want them to be...agreeable, yielding, and physically available. So the cliché that 'girls want love and guys want sex' gets down to a pretty basic and understandable game of control between a guy and a girl with chemistry!"

"Annie, do you think a relationship like this could work? It seems like you'd have two people who are attracted to each other and talk freely and openly. And, if they had a Basis, they might decide to become partners in marriage. It sounds great, but I'm wondering if any of us could ever get that mature?"

"Jennah, where is the other way getting us? There's even more," I added without a pause. "Because they'd found enough in common to build a life together, and they'd think the other person's freedom is important, and they'd speak their mind with love that thinks of others...just imagine! They wouldn't demand responses from each other, though they could still ask or invite each other to do or say something they'd like. This couple could focus on loving the other person more than being loved. They would still have many hopes, and decisions would have to be made, but it wouldn't be about controlling each other!"

"Just one more thing," Jennah winked. "Can we girls talk about this stuff this openly? I mean, shouldn't we just get a manicure and talk about who should be dating whom?"

"Probably, but maybe we could give our daughters a little more than that!" I winked back as I headed to my apartment.

I left that conversation with Jennah feeling like the sails were up and the wind was behind me. I couldn't wait to get back to my journal as my thoughts were starting to swirl in great numbers.

Journal

That's it! Another key part of God's design for how relating works. The key for teens (and adults) is to first learn to Tell the Truth with Love and allow others the freedom to respond as they please! I'll call this Agenda-less Relating...no, Control-Free-Relating. Control-Free-Relating means that we do not have a plan or idea for how the other person should respond in a conversation. They are free & uncontrolled...just like I'd like others to be with me (Golden Rule). They don't have a "job" to make me "happy." In Control-Free-Relating you are not trying to want to hear or act a way you want them to be. Together we are discovering the conversation...so we REALLY get to know each other! My goal is not to affirm their freedom to be and do what they want. (even if I don't like it!)

SUMMARY

Chemistry + Basis + Truth + Love + Freedom
(or minus Control) = Control-Free (Authentic) Relating

The key for teens (and adults) is to first learn to Tell the
Truth with Love and allow others the freedom to respond
as they please!

I believe this is a real discovery: The most important skill for success in relationships is Control-Free-Relating.

Isn't this the very thing most people don't do? Usually people focus on the response of the other person or what they themselves are calculating to say, rather than working together. Working together will allow two people (or more) to get to really know each other.

I started this journey believing that using the right process would bring about success or failure in relationships. When we begin dating or courting, don't we have all kinds of expectations for the other person...usually from our own selfish plotting? I guess there still could be some kind of process, but it must be one that only comes into play when we quit trying to control the relationship!

Control-Free-Relating is best experienced where at least two people, without any requirements for the conversation at all, simply speak the truth with love (Golden Rule) to one another.

NOTE: Control-Free-Relating must also be the answer to Glaen's question about married couples who don't have good chemistry. Control-Free-Relating must be the catalyst he mentioned. A catalyst affects the chemical reaction without being changed itself. Telling the truth with love changes the relationship, but it doesn't change the truth!

Maybe I should state this as a lie:
<u>Lie #6</u>

If we act just the right way and say just the right things, we can get the approval of others and they'll respond the way we want them to.

Countering Truth
Speaking the truth with love is the center piece of effective relating because it starts with your freedom and ends with theirs.

"Goodnight Glaen," I thought as I turned in with all these thoughts at play in my mind. "You certainly have me seeing with fresh eyes."

SUMMARY

Control-Free-Relating is where at least two people, without any requirements for the conversation at all, simply speak the truth with love (Golden Rule) to one another.

SUMMARY

<u>Lie #6</u>

If we act just the right way and say just the right things, we can get the approval of others and they'll respond the way we want them to.

<u>Countering Truth</u>

Speaking the truth with love is the centerpiece of effective relating because it starts with your freedom and ends with theirs.

"OK, I've got a 30 minute break, now what do you want to talk to me about?" Jake said as he straddled a chair and set his Dasanti bottle down on the table.

"Jake, I don't want to talk to you, I want to talk WITH you," I said.

"OK, what do you want to talk WITH me about?" he retorted.

"Jake," I continued on, "I think I've discovered a real secret to relating and relationships; and, it involves not talking ABOUT anything."

"OK, I give," Jake said as he looked at me with thinning patience.

"I call it Control-Free-Relating," I started.

"Sounds official," Jake offered.

"I think it is, Jake. Most of the time don't we all have goals for how the other person should respond to us? You come up to the table with the goal of taking my order, and then I talk to you with the goal of getting what I want to drink or eat. At other times guys and girls have different goals. It may be a goal to get a date, or to get a compliment, or to get help from a friend. Most of the time these goals aren't a big deal, but they can pretty easily turn into monsters. The monster shows up when we impose EXPECTATIONS on others."

"Hmm…," Jake said as he winked at me. "Like if I expect you to get to the point and you tell me lots of random details?"

"Exactly," I said smiling back. "Let's say I'm going on and on without telling you the point. How would you respond if you really did expect the point?"

"I'd probably get a little irritated and ask you to get to the point," he answered as he moved two of his fingers in a circular motion between us, as to say, "Hurry up!"

"That's right, you'd be irritated," I said. "Then, what if I expected you to patiently let me tell you my story with all of the detail I thought you needed?"

"I guess you'd get irritated with my impatience and this little get-to-the-point hand signal," Jake said.

"And it would just keep going," I insisted. "Jake, this is how it goes with fights between people. They impose goals and expectations on each other. They insist the other person understand and agree with them; or, they expect the other person to be polite, or silent, in the way he responds. Actually, they can have a million expectations. It's like giving the other person a job to do; and if he doesn't do it, then look out!"

"OK, so what is Control-Free-Relating?" Jake asked.

"It's what I want to try with you right now," I said as I asked him with my eyes.

"How do we play, Annie?" Jake asked.

"Well, it goes like this," I began.

I explained to Jake that my idea was that we both decide up front to allow the other person to say anything they want to say. Next, we allow the conversation to go anywhere it wants to go. No response or conversation was OK, too. I stated that it was not purposeless. The purpose is to pursue real relating, to know each other, or at least to hear each other. But the path to the purpose was to not really have any goal or demand for the other person's response. We could just speak honestly (ideally with the Golden Rule in mind, of course). We could go anywhere we wanted to…but nothing has to go anywhere.

"Jake, in this sense it's Control-Free-Relating because neither of us will be trying to control, demand, fix, etc., what the other one is saying," I concluded.

All these years later I still look back on that first 25 minute conversation as the most incredible one of my life. Of course, I've enjoyed Control-Free-Relating a thousand times since then, but that moment was the first, and the most memorable.

"I'll start. You have really pretty eyes," Jake said.

"Stop it, be serious," were the first words I ever uttered in a Control-Free-Relating conversation.

"Oh, so I am required to be serious?" Jake asked.

"Oops, sorry," I said.

"You have the most incredibly beautiful eyes. They have that deep sparkle I've only seen in a few people. It's a sparkle that says you are really awake and your spirit is actively reaching for the things it wants. I have that look occasionally, but I'm a little too cautious to really hold on to it," Jake poured out.

"Hmm…," I said. "My Mother is like that too, but she seemed to close her eyes a few years ago. I think it was something about aging and leaving the theatre because she got pregnant."

"I didn't know your mother ever had a baby," Jake said.

We both laughed.

"No really, she was in the theatre?" he asked.

"She was grand; at least they tell me she was. I know we were fascinated with the stories she would read to us as kids. It often felt like the book she was holding was in our way. We just wanted to dash with Mom into the world she was visiting," I answered.

Time slowed down and Jake and I talked about nothing, for years, in those 25 minutes.

"I've got to get back to work. Let's try this again sometime over dinner." He smiled and waited.

"Please," I said in a pretty uncharacteristic way.

"So that was what it's like?" I thought. What a surprising experience to sit and allow a conversation to blossom. I strolled back home with a newfound sense of freedom I had never known. It was all the more clear that people fight because they chain relationships to goals of their own making, rather than trusting God or His designs for the outcome. I guessed that was what Dad was trying to tell me that night on the phone. He had given up being himself because of the goal he had for mother; as a result he wasn't in a real relationship anymore because Dad himself wasn't there. Love must be pretty easy to cover up, or to uncover, depending on how honest two people can be with each other.

"Lord," I prayed. "Please help me learn how to keep this freedom at the top of my priorities with others, and to leave goals for others out of my relationships as often as possible. Amen."

At that moment Galatians 5:1 jumped into my mind:

It was for freedom that Christ set us free...

"Hey, Jenn. What's up?" I said as I picked up the phone.

"Oh, not really anything," she said.

"So how's Steve," I said as usual.

"He's doing OK...," she said as I interrupted.

"Jenn, I can't tell you how much you've helped my book by trying Control-Free-Relating with Steve. Glaen said it sounded great; and just for me personally, it was wonderful to hear how you started telling the truth and Steve opened up his heart without you complaining. And the part where you keep silent...and let him talk...well that was miraculous!" I stopped because of Jennah's tears.

"Jennah, are you crying?"

"Oh, Annie," she said as she started into deep sobs.

"What is it?" I asked.

"We blew it," she said in a whisper.

"What do you mean you blew it? Is the relationship over because of really relating?" was the only question I could think to ask. "I mean, it's good to know now if it wasn't a match."

"Annie, we related fine; in fact, we related too well," Jennah said.

"You mean you had sex?" I said as I was starting to get the picture.

"Oh Annie," she whispered again.

"Jennah, we are so clear on this one. You and I had studied and prayed and decided to wait for our husbands."

"I think he is going to be my husband!" Jenn shot back.

"But Jenn, we are Christians," I said.
After a long pause I told her, "Look Sweetie, I'm your friend and God's forgiveness, love, and understanding are bigger than this; tell me what happened."

"I know, thanks for your friendship," she said. "Annie, we didn't really have sex, but we might as well have."

"OK, I don't want those details, I just want to hear what led up to it," I said.

"Well," she began. "We've been falling more and more in love; and before you say anything, I want you to know it wasn't at all like any relationship I've ever had. I don't even think I have to have Steve…I really just hope he'll have me. I've never known a guy like I know him."

"Well, I knew you two were talking about serious stuff," I affirmed.

"True," she continued. "About three weeks ago Steve made it clear, and I agreed, that dating without the possibility of marriage was a bad idea. You remember, we had gone back home for the weekend; well, Steve and my dad went up to the lake house to work on the boat. During that time, Steve talked to my dad about us and asked if Dad approved of us seriously dating. Dad told Steve he didn't know how such things worked since he and Mom eloped. They talked about dating and courting and God; I can't believe Steve was that brave, but apparently they had a great conversation and Dad gave Steve his blessing."

"OK, so why are you crying?" I asked.

"I just feel like I've been given this great gift, to finally be truthful without demanding another person to respond a certain way; and now I've misused it," she said.

"Jennah, I may be crazy, but it sounds like you've proved it," I pointed out. "If you and Steve grow intimate, wouldn't it show up in the physical area?"

"I guess," she said.

"Well, it sounds like we just need to realize that Control-Free-Relating is a powerful way to connect. The desire for intimacy can be a struggle for us who want to save our bodies for our husbands; but it could also be a great part of our lives once we're married," I said, a little surprised that I made that much sense.

"So now what?" Jennah asked.

"Jenn, before we answer that, can I ask some questions?"

"Sure Annie, that's what I signed up for."

"First," I said, "We learned a lot about definitions."

"Right," Jennah replied.

"You said you and Steve were 'falling more and more in love.' What do you mean by 'falling in love'?" I asked.

"Well it means deep feelings. Wanting to be together. Missing each other. A lot of, you know, sparks when we are together."

"So when you looked in his eyes…," I started.

"Yes."

"And when you brushed against each other…and when you talk…"

"Of course," Jennah cut me off. "Oh Annie, I wish so much that I could have those days back. I am not sure if the damage can ever be undone."

"Maybe it can't, Jennah, but based on what we've learned about relationships, there is only one thing to do now," I paused.

"I guess it's to focus on the present," Jennah said. "No, I know that's right," Jennah stated firmly.

"So what can we learn from this, and what do you do now?" I asked.

Jennah explained she learned, as the chemistry grew between them, that she and Steve assumed they were committed and the future together was guaranteed. So, they acted married. Everyone else acted that way toward them too; and before they knew it, physical intimacy raced ahead of their convictions and consciences.

"The only thing is, Annie, this was more powerful than anything I've ever experienced."

"So how does Steve feel about sex before marriage?" I asked.

"I think Steve is even more broken about this than I am. I know we also want our honeymoon to really mean something, and I think his commitment to a Christ-based marriage stopped us from…"

"I get it, Jenn. Sounds like your next Control-Free-Relating session will have a little more purpose than usual! I think you both just need to make a decision together."

"Pray for me Annie," she said. "You can count on it," I answered.

After we hung up I wrote down a new observation:

> **Freedom is risky, because freedom means there is real choice.**

The truth of the risk didn't change my mind about anything, because freedom and truth are worth all the risks in the world.

The morning was beautiful. Spring was giving way to summer as the semester was coming to a close. As I left for class I checked my mail and opened a note from Mom.

Annie,

> I just wanted to send you a note before you heard anything from someone else. I met with your father briefly today because we needed to sign a few legal papers. I can't tell you how different he seemed; it was like I remembered him back in college. As we visited, he invited me to go to lunch just to talk. It's really strange, but I accepted...and well...I wanted you to know. Please pray for us to have a good relationship...and don't go crazy expecting too much!

Love,
Mom

P.S. Have a great day!

I went to the classroom early that day. Glaen was due any moment. I had never taken the time to soak in the room itself. It wasn't fancy, but it was old. Old, that is, in the sense that it had history and time in it. Wooden floors and a desk on a raised platform, traditional blackboard with low set windows; all glancing to the ivy-framed courtyard of Dole-Emerson Hall, the Fine Arts building of this faithful old university. The Dole family had employed their fortunes to establish the school and community as a Christian banner of education. Despite the drift of colleges, it had held on to a spirit of goodness you could still see today. Degrees remain in Bible and theology, campus ministries flourish, and the Chapel is maintained and open twenty-four-seven as a quiet and safe place to gather your thoughts and talk to the Lord.

"Hello Annie," a voice startled me from behind.

"Hi Glaen," I returned. "I didn't hear you come in."

"I was quiet," he said. "I didn't want to interrupt your thoughts about this room."

"How did you know what I was thinking about?" I asked.

"Annie, you'd be surprised what I know. For example, you haven't solved the mystery about romance, but you have tasted how to unhand your expectations of others," Glaen said with a bright glimmer in both eyes and a smile that insisted that everything was on course.

I suddenly felt a different way toward Glaen. At times he had been a mentor and a father to me, but at other times I wanted his qualities in a husband. Just then, however, I was afraid and hopeful all at once. I didn't want to say a word, and looking into his clear expression insisted my eyes look away.

"Annie, I've brought you the book I promised," Glaen began.

Glaen slowly unraveled a sheer white cloth with ancient emblems on it to reveal a book. He handed it to me and stepped away. What I held was the most disturbing thing I had ever seen in my life.

"There are very specific instructions about that book. Please look at me and listen to my words," Glaen began. "You have been given a gift few of your kind receive in this life. All of this comes as an answer to your prayer. The book has the exact insight you have been seeking and I have borrowed it for one hour. You may take any notes you like and read as much of it as you wish. There is only one restriction; you cannot leave this room with the book. I'll be back for it in one hour."

I couldn't think what to say or what to ask before he was gone. I just stared at the book for a few moments. The title was _The Artful Science of Love: A Fieldbook for Life-Long Relationships._ The shocking part was that it had MY NAME as the author!

I thumbed through the book and saw my journal entries and the principles I had discovered. There was a chapter entitled, "Isaac Newton and the Laws of Love." I was looking at a completed book from all the coursework I had done for Glaen.

My first thought was that he had somehow taken my notes and edited them into a book. I wasn't sure if he was trying to surprise me or torture me. But of one thing I was sure; there was a chapter before my eyes which I had not written a word about. Its title was "The Romance Trap." Suddenly I woke up and started taking notes furiously.

"Of course!" I kept saying. "That makes sense."

Before my eyes, I was reading the answers about romance and the sometimes terrible damage it can do to relationships. I also saw the better way, the way relationships which are unchained by the "romance trap" can truly work every single day of a couple's life.

"Oh no, the clock!" There was no way I could finish. Twenty minutes were left and there were so many other things I wanted to copy from the book. Glaen had long since left my mind, and all I could think about was keeping the book.

"Twenty minutes," I thought. "That's five minutes to the Copy Center…ten minutes to copy…five minutes to get back. I can do it!"

I dashed past the quadrangle, the library, and Polmier's; but the Copy Center had a line five students deep. I quickly begged the whole group to let me break to the front of the line, but someone said, "Hey, we're all in a hurry!" I didn't have time to lecture them on human decency, instead I simply said, "I'll buy you all the drink of your choice at Polmier's…just tell Jake that Annie is treating the five of you from the Copy Center." For one long minute they all looked at the floor, then looked at each other, and then looked at me.

"It's a deal," the guy at the front of the line said. And with that they ALL left for the Coffee Shoppe!

"May I help you?" the girl behind the counter said as I stared at the whole group of newfound friends as they walked out.

"Yes, could you please copy this as quickly as possible?" I said handing her the book.

"Sure, but you gave them all a free drink at Polmier's for this?" she asked.

I looked at the book and feared I was losing my mind. The book no longer had the title, or my name, or the words inside.

Suddenly it was just a bound set of empty pages, like a journal before you write one word. Had I made this up? Was I just caught in a dream? I decided to dash back to the classroom, maybe Glaen would be there and would forgive me for my foolishness. Or, maybe he would tell me I made the whole thing up.

I got to the room five minutes late; no Glaen. I sat down and caught my breath while I hoped and waited for Glaen.

"My notes!" I blurted aloud. "Please be there," I begged. I opened my journal and turned to the last creased page. There in a dark box were the words I'd copied down earlier: "The Romance Trap." They were there and not a word was missing! The book Glaen had given me was still blank, but my notes, thank God, had not been erased.

Just then I noticed a small embossed note card on a nearby desk. In raised letters across the top it said, "GLAEN." A single feather was attached, and in perfect handwriting was the following rhyme:

A prayer away
The answer tell,
The messenger hears,
The Olde Chapel

I had no idea what it meant. It could have been something he dropped, or something he left for me. I did know that Glaen did nothing by accident and he would find me like he did before. On the other hand I couldn't wait to show Jake what I now knew about romance...plus I had to pay for five mocha-frappuccinos anyway.

"There, fifteen dollars and 56 cents," I said as I handed Jake the money. "Now, come sit down and let me share with you what I just learned about romance: Jake, it's a trap!" I whispered.

"Hey, Annie," he said. "Now what was the Copy Center generosity about?"

"Oh, I'll tell you later," I said as I thought it was best I keep Glaen and the book a secret until I knew a few things for sure.

"OK," Jake said. "Let me get this next order filled and I'll take a break to hear about this 'romance trap.'"

As I sat at a back table I decided to follow a hunch and make a phone call. "Yes, Registrar's Office please," I said. "Hi, I was wondering; could you tell me the time and room number of a class? It's called Original Non-Fiction, ONF 101, and it's taught by Glaen Breuch."

A few moments later the lady came back on the line and said, "I'm sorry I can't find either a class or a professor by those names. In fact, in my forty years here I've never heard of that class; but it sounds interesting."

"Maybe they'll offer it someday. Well, thanks anyway," I said. Could it be that Glaen really was an answer to prayer, an...?

"So tell me," Jake said as I jumped out of my skin.

"You scared me to death," I said.

"Sorry, you looked like you had seen a ghost even before I came up behind you."

"That's pretty close to accurate, Jake," I said. "Now let me tell you about romance."

"First Jake, describe to me what romance is normally said to be about," I began.

"Well, let's see," he said. "The speakers I've heard always say you should never quit dating your wife. By that they mean that women need to be showered with special gifts and trips; you know, carnations, candy, Cancun."

"That's right and it's a trap," I stated flatly.

"You mean there's something wrong with showering a girl you love with gifts?"

"Yes!" I said.

"Wow, Annie, you're going to be the ideal wife for someone," Jake winked.

"No, I don't mean that those things are bad in themselves; but they trap people into a cycle that moves them away from a real relationship," I said. "Jake, I've noticed that over time, 'romance' is at the heart of a lot of conflict between couples."

With that Jake broke out into a pretty good imitation of Neil Diamond singing "You Don't Send Me Flowers."

"Actually that's the idea," I said. "What is it that romance is all about…in one word?"

"I'd say it's the word, 'special,'" he answered.

"How about 'unusual,'" I offered.

"Well, that word works too," Jake admitted.

"Jake, here's the point," I said triumphantly. "Romance is about the unusual, or the exciting. It invites a standard for love that demands doing creative and unique things to truly show or prove love. It's a trap because it works like saltwater for thirst.

The more you drink it, the thirstier you get...until you die! Once the relationship is all about romance, then complaints and problems will start growing; and the measure of the relationship will be 'romance.' Each cycle invites doing something 'special,' and usually it must be more special than the last time. People begin to feel romance is the cure for any relationship woes. Jake, how much time do you think most couples spend on romance; and I mean the ones who work at it?"

"Oh, I'd say about ten percent of the time," he guessed.

"Very generous," I replied. "Even with ten percent, ninety percent of the relationship is never about the unusual; it's about the mundane, common, day-to-day stuff that makes up a life together. If the relationship is about the 'usual' then that is where the relating is going to happen. When we think about romance as the key, then we are inviting ourselves to miss out on the real opportunity."

"You know Annie," Jake added as he rubbed his chin. "I heard a Pastor who had lost his wife to cancer tell us this same point. He said that what he missed most about his wife was not the trips they had taken, but the times they had laughed in the backyard over iced tea. He said he wished he could just take the top off a new pickle jar for her one more time."

"That's exactly the point," I said. "*Romance is a trap because the best relationships are not about the exciting and unusual; instead, they are about connecting together in the common day-to-day world.*"

"That's cool. I think you've got something there," he said. "Now, does it mean that all romance is bad?"

"Well, no," I said. "We all like special things, but we need to realize what they are about. A vacation is special. A trip is special. However, when we live for those things, kind of like the dream most people have about retirement, we miss out on most of what life is really about. I want to be treated in special ways, but I no longer want to make the special treatment a standard or expectation. Most high school and college girls spend their energy trying to get guys to constantly treat them as though they are princesses…the result is that they never really learn how to relate without also trying to control."

"You know Annie, romance might be a trap for another reason," Jake offered.

"How's that?" I asked.

"Well, when we are honest, especially us guys, we basically buy into the whole Hollywood package. Hollywood, and the world, tells us that love is sex. What else does 'make love' mean?"

"Good point Jake," I said a little uncomfortable.

"So, it seems that Hollywood's view of romance is that it should, and will, lead to sex. I mean, according to the pop-view, isn't the point about having a 'romantic evening' all about winding up in the sack? For most guys, a 'romantic evening' that ends with a peck-on-the-cheek and an 'Oh I had a wonderful evening' would be the ultimate letdown," Jake said emphatically.

"So romantic dating or courting winds up 'playing married,' but with the excitement of 'making love' at the end of the evening," I added.

"I think that's about...."

"Wait," I interrupted. "Girls want a romantic man to 'sweep them off their feet,' which I guess has always meant being carried off to bed?"

"How about a corollary?" Jake asked.

"Since romance is about the unusual and exciting, sex is the highest aim of romance."

"I think that's awesome!" I added.

Jake and I sat there for a long quiet moment before I showed him Glaen's card. "What do you make of this?" I said.

A prayer away
The answer tell,
The messenger hears,
The Olde Chapel

"I don't know," Jake said as he looked at the card. "It seems like the odd thing here is the word Olde. Delo, oeld, lode…."

"What are you doing?" I said.

"Oh, I always play 'jumbles' with words. It's sort of a habit to see what they spell. Like your name 'annie' spells nanie, innae, enina, anina, ainen, et cetera."

"Jake, that's it!" I suddenly realized. "Olde spells D-O-L-E. It's the Dole Chapel! I'm sorry, I've got to run."

I knew Glaen would be at the Chapel. It made perfect sense.

SUMMARY

Romance is a trap because true relationships are not about the exciting and unusual; instead, true relationships are about connecting together in the common day-to-day world.

Romance Corollary: Since romance is about the unusual and exciting, sex is the highest aim of romance.

The Chapel was built in 1888 as the first building on campus. Its polished wood and arching stained glass windows made it a world unlike any other at the university. It had pews and an old-fashioned flavor that always felt like a place God really accepted. I walked in with the low lights and slight echo from my heels on the stone floor.

"Hello?" I said. "Glaen? Anybody?"

The Chapel was empty so I sat down a little disheartened. "What in the world was going on?" I thought to myself. I had this strange course with a strange professor, and more insights than I ever imagined about relationships. But, the one person I wanted to relate to right then wasn't around. It seemed right to pray.

"Lord," I said. "I know you are the Sovereign over the universe You made. I know that You created us to relate to You and to each other...and, I know You've helped me see things that others would benefit from knowing. I know there are guys and girls in high school, college, and the work-world who need to know these things. I pray that You let them know; and, it doesn't have to be through me. Lord, I also ask that You let me see Glaen again, and that he'll forgive me for taking the book out of the room."

At that moment the lights flickered and the wind sang outside around the columns of the Dole Chapel.

"Hello Annie," a voice said softly and safely from the shadows behind the vestry. He stepped out and I could see him, it was Glaen.

"Glaen, you came!" I said as I rushed up to hug him. "I'm so sorry I didn't follow your instructions, please forgive me."

"Annie, there is nothing to forgive. You made a choice and something happened; life is mostly that same story."

"I know," I said as I pulled out the book from under my jacket. "Here's your book back."

"Annie, it isn't mine, it's yours," he said. "Look!" as he pointed to the book in my hands.

I was now holding the original book; it was all there just as I had seen it in the classroom earlier that day.

"I don't understand," I told Glaen.

"Annie, one day you prayed to understand relationships. It pleased those in authority over me to answer your prayer and to offer you the opportunity to give these insights to a needy human race. You accepted the offer and wrote the book. I borrowed it so you could read your own insights in the one place you were stuck: romance."

"So you are an answer to prayer…and…you borrowed the book from me in the future?" I murmured as I caught myself with the edge of the pew. Glaen caught my arm and lifted me up.

"Yes, Annie," Glaen said.

"Now, here's your commission: write your book on relationships while you practice the principles for ten years. We want you to truly experience and refine your own understanding before you publish it. Annie, this kind of genuine relating is a skill to develop. First, understand it, and then practice it. In time it will be as natural as walking."

"But Glaen, people need this now!" I argued.

"True, but they already know and experience most of these truths; and, Annie, it is better to give an answer you truly know than one you just know about. In any event, there is already a book that instructs people how to do this. It is your opportunity to help them understand how to read it. It's your choice, but you know how we work," Glaen winked at me as he extended his hand."

"May I have the book? I only borrowed it and the author wants it back," he said as he winked at me.

I handed Glaen the book and turned as the door to the Chapel opened. It was Jake.

"Annie, what's so important in here?"

"Jake," I said with an introductory hand motion. "I'd like you to meet Glaen."

"O...K," Jake said with the slow voice that you might use with a mentally unstable person.

Glaen was gone! I fumbled around and found words to get away from Glaen.

"I'm sorry for running out, but I needed to pray," I said. "Jake, it's been the most incredible day! Everything's great! Thanks for following me here."

I couldn't help but think what a great friend Jake had been over these months and, for the first time, I was open to a relationship. I didn't want to date, or court, or get married. I just wanted to relate with a guy I liked, and be OK with wherever it might go. I just wasn't sure Jake was up for it.

"No problem, Annie," he said. "I just wanted to make sure you were OK."

After a long pause, Jake added a few words that opened my heart.

"I was thinking about all you said about romance and Control-Free-Relating on the way over here, and it brought to mind something my Granddad told me. At his fiftieth wedding anniversary I asked him how he and Granny did it…stayed together so long. 'It's simple,' he said. 'First, we married for keeps. Second, we made it a priority always to do two things: **Drop the Past & Tell the Truth.**' It reminded me a lot of what you showed me from your journal one day, '**Truth is the lifeblood of real relationships.**'"

"Jake," I asked. "Do you know how to work a DVD player?"

SUMMARY

Drop the Past & Tell the Truth.

–or–

Truth is the lifeblood of real relationships.

Today I'm thirty-eight and I'm holding in my hand the same book I held over fifteen years ago; a new box just arrived from the publisher. The smell of a fresh book with the smell of my home gave me the taste of joy I had hoped to know on this day.

The doorbell rang and I opened it. "Hi, please come in!" I said. I knew it had been minutes for him, but ages for me. "Glaen, how I've wanted to see you!"

"Annie, you've progressed well and you have been faithful with the book, your family, and your ministry among the high school girls at church," he said. "How are you?"

"I am wonderful, and grateful for all I've been given. Glaen, even the tragedies have lessons and purpose in them. I now see how Mom's and Dad's divorce allowed my Dad to find himself, and uncover her love for him again. I see how breaking up with Jake, and his response, got me happily married. Once you left fifteen years ago, I gathered to my heart just how un-alone I really was…like I'm being watched over," I winked at him.

"Yes, Annie," Glaen smiled. "Class is always in session; people merely need to be open and take good notes."

"Here's the book, now go tell me to take good notes," I smiled and hugged Glaen as I put it in his hands. "Will I ever see you again?"

Glaen said, "I'm late," and disappeared.

Immediately the phone rang, "Hi, honey," I said. "Yes, the books are here. They do look great, and it is amazing that we are in our third printing! Now? Celebrate me as an author—again? With the kids at the Pizza Barn? You are such a romantic fool…I'd love to! See you there." I hung up the phone and laughed, "Jake for a husband was an even better gift."

It still amazes me that Jake threw away my "break up" letter and continued to tell the truth about his hopes for us…I'd never had anyone call me on my silly bluff. I realize now how providential that was. In order to feel secure with a man, I needed to know he was fine without me, but still wanted me. And even though that is exactly the same thing that my dad did with my mom, it still was lost on me until years later.

I stay amazed that well after I finished the book, and after we had decided our relationship should move toward marriage, that I noticed Jake was ahead of me in applying the principles I'd discovered.

Jake suggested that we could share our mutual value of seeking selflessness as the first part of our Basis for a life together. Our wedding bands contain this verse:

> Let nothing be done through selfish ambition or conceit, but
> in lowliness of mind let each esteem others better than
> himself. Let each of you look out not only for his own
> interests, but also for the interests of others.
> (Philippians 2:3-4)

We meet Jennah and Steve every year at Jennah's parents' lake house; and Krista...well, this isn't a fairy tale!

After Glaen had gone I sat there dazed for a moment thinking about what unimaginable gifts I had already received in this life, when I noticed a card on the floor. It was Glaen's embossed stationary with writing in his beautiful script:

> *Anne,*
> *Writing is a generosity, too...*

On the back of the card was a snow-white feather and another
one of his rhymes:

> The Olde Chapel
>   Works the same;
> Messenger truly
>   Is my name.
>   - Glaen Breuch

"Well look at that; G…l…a…e…n. I never noticed,"
I said as I put the note in my Bible and got my car keys.
"Let's celebrate."

Study Guide to Glaen:
A study guide and other resources for teachers and small group leaders of the powerful principles found in Glaen are available at **www.glaen.com**

Other books by Fred R. Lybrand:

Preaching On Your Feet (Broadman & Holman Publishing, 2008)
"Preaching on your feet" describes a unique but age-old method of pulpit communication. In layman's terms, it involves being "in the moment," not solely relying on pre-written notes (though they can still be helpful), and staying open to what God might have in store during any given preaching appointment. It all adds up to a heart-to-heart style of delivery that makes preaching a joy for both the orator and listener time and again. Aspiring and veteran pastors and teachers alike will find much to consider and implement in this refreshing new volume on public speaking.

Back to Faith: Reclaiming Gospel Clarity in an Age of Incongruence (Xulon Press, 2009)
Are you worried about knowing if a loved-one who believed in Christ by faith alone, but who fell away from the faith, could still greet you in heaven? Do you find some Christians busily judging the eternal destiny of others based on works rather than by faith in Christ alone...but don't know how to biblically invite them to stop it? Back to Faith is a resource that lays to rest the conflict between faith and works and the confusion about James 2.
It gives back the full confidence all believers can enjoy in the gracious and finished work of Christ; all enjoyed by faith alone.